The

ULTIMATE PALEO CLEANSE

4 Weeks of Fabulous Paleo Recipes

The
ULTIMATE PALEO CLEANSE

—— AMELIA SIMONS ——

Skyhorse Publishing

Skyhorse Publishing books may be purchased in bulk at special discounts for sales promotion, corporate gifts, fund-raising, or educational purposes. Special editions can also be created to specifications. For details, contact the Special Sales Department, Skyhorse Publishing, 307 West 36th Street, 11th Floor, New York, NY 10018 or info@skyhorsepublishing.com.

Skyhorse® and Skyhorse Publishing® are registered trademarks of Skyhorse Publishing, Inc.®, a Delaware corporation.

Visit our website at www.skyhorsepublishing.com.

10 9 8 7 6 5 4 3 2 1

Library of Congress Cataloging-in-Publication Data is available on file.

Cover design by Jane Sheppard
Cover photo credit Thinkstock

Print ISBN: 978-1-62914-552-5

Printed in China

Table of Contents

INTRODUCTION – PALEOLITHIC PRIMER

What is Paleolithic?

The Paleolithic way of eating includes various names, like Primal Diet, Cave Man Diet, Stone Age Diet, Hunter-Gatherer Diet, the Paleo Diet™ and a few others. Basically, the Paleolithic way of eating consists of a low-carb diet that attempts to imitate what our ancestors ate before farming and other advancements changed our diets.

As with many other ways of eating, there are some variation and degrees of limitations practiced by those who try to eat like our "primal" ancestors did. With that said, what follows are the basic guidelines that most proponents of the Paleolithic way of eating agree upon.

Whether you fully embrace this way of eating by going "cold turkey," or ease your way gently into the program, here are some basic guidelines.

What Foods are "Off Limits?"

Refined Sugars: Basically, the rule is to avoid all sugars. These include white sugar, high fructose corn syrup, candy, milk chocolate, soda, and artificial sweeteners. Some spokespersons for Paleolithic eating allow small amounts of raw honey, pure maple syrup, and coconut sugar, but also advise these sugars to be an occasional treat.

Grains: The types of grain to avoid include wheat, rye, barley, rice, oats, and corn. Foods to eliminate from your diet include bread, pasta, baked goods, pancakes, biscuits, muffins, bagels, and cereals. Grains are high in carbohydrates and are calorie-dense.

Legumes: This category includes beans of all kinds, peas, lentils, soybeans, tofu, soy products, and peanuts.

Dairy Products: Try to exclude dairy products like regular milk, cream, fruit yogurts, ice cream, and processed cheeses.

♦ While many in the Paleolithic community avoid dairy, others do not. If you can tolerate dairy and want to enjoy it on occasion, start with cultured butter, Greek yogurt (not fruit flavored), kefir, clotted milks, and aged cheeses. These are fermented products that drastically reduce the lactose (milk sugar) levels.

♦ Next would come raw, high-fat dairy like raw butter and cream because they are minimally processed and are good sources of saturated fat. Most of these are free from lactose and casein and should come from grass-fed, pasture-fed animals.

♦ Avoid homogenized and pasteurized milk. If you must buy it, make it organic, hormone- and antibiotic-free milk. Because nuts are allowed, consider substituting unsweetened almond milk and coconut milk in place of cow's milk.

♦ Grass-fed butter is considered OK. If you want to eat cheese on occasion, too, be sure they are aged cheeses because aging drastically reduces the levels of lactose and casein.

Some Meats: Avoid processed meats like hot dogs, bologna, and lunch meats. If eating bacon and sausage, try to eat those without nitrates and nitrites. The bacon issue is still widely debated among the Paleo community—some believe it is okay if using nitrite/nitrate-free bacon that is also sugar-free. Others believe because it is cured, it is not allowed. The choice is yours!

Oils: Avoid anything "partially hydrogenated:" shortening, margarines, canola oil, soybean oil, cottonseed oil, peanut oil, corn oil, and sunflower oil. Note: be sure to check the label on your mayonnaise.

What Foods are Allowed?

Meats, Seafood, and Eggs: Meats, seafood, and eggs are perhaps the most important components of the Paleolithic Diet. These include beef, pork, lamb, bison, poultry, shrimp, crab, trout, salmon, mackerel, and other wild-caught fish, including sardines, plus oysters, mussels, and clams. Once again, bacon and sausage are widely debated so you decide if they are okay for you or not.

Vegetables: Vegetables are greatly encouraged and can be eaten in unlimited quantities. Focus on leafy greens of all kinds. Whether to include potatoes and other starchy tubers in your diet is an area of varying opinions at this point.

Fruits: Fruits are allowed but should be limited, especially if you need to lose weight. High sugar fruits like dried fruits and juices should be included only occasionally.

Nuts and Seeds: Nuts and seeds are generally allowed. They are high in fat so limit your intake if you want to lose weight. Nuts and seeds include macadamias, Brazil nuts, hazelnuts, pistachios, walnuts, almonds, pecans, cashews, squash seeds, sunflower seeds, and pumpkin seeds. Note: Peanuts are legumes and are not allowed.

Healthy Fats: Olive oil and nut oils like coconut oil are generally encouraged. Butter, palm oil, ghee, and animal fats are on the allowable list.

Beverages: All spokespersons agree that water is best and should be your main drink. Generally, tea is considered to be fine, while there continue to be some variations concerning coffee and alcohol. Beverages that require sweetening by sugars or artificial sweeteners are discouraged.

Throughout this collection of recipes (and the others in my series), I have tried to guide you into this way of eating. The goal is to make positive changes toward this way of eating without making you feel like it has to be one certain way. Simply know your labels and use your best judgment.

If you cannot afford organic or grass-fed beef, do not fret about that. Just buy the basic ingredients and follow the basic guidelines for eating Paleolithic style.

I hope you enjoy this collection of Paleolithic breakfast recipes. They are some of my family's absolute favorites!

BREAKFASTS

Frittatas & Egg Dishes

GARDEN FRESH FRITTATA

Ingredients:

- 8 eggs
- ¼ cup almond milk
- Salt and pepper to taste
- 2 tablespoons olive oil
- 2–3 garlic cloves, finely chopped or crushed
- 2 cups baby spinach, chopped or shredded
- 1 red onion, chopped
- ½ cup fresh mushrooms, sliced
- 1 red bell pepper, sliced or chunked
- 2 tablespoons fresh parsley, if desired

Directions:

1. Preheat your oven to 425°F.
2. In a separate bowl, combine the eggs and almond milk.
3. Mix well and set aside.
4. Place an oven-safe, medium-sized skillet over medium heat and pour in the olive oil.
5. Once the oil is heated, place the garlic, spinach, red onion, fresh mushrooms, and red bell pepper into the skillet.
6. Cook the vegetables for 3 to 4 minutes, until they are tender.
7. Slowly add in the egg/almond mixture to the vegetables in the skillet and turn the heat down to low.
8. Cook over low heat for approximately 10 minutes.
9. Once the edges look firm, place the oven-safe skillet into your preheated oven.
10. Cook for 15 to 20 minutes.
11. The frittata will be done when the center is firm and no longer jiggles.
12. Top the frittata with fresh parsley and cut into wedges.
13. Serve hot and enjoy.

VEGGIE FRITTATA

Ingredients:

- 1 cup broccoli florets, diced
- ½ cup chopped red onion
- 1 yellow summer squash, diced
- 1 cup cooked meat, diced
- ½ cup sun-dried tomatoes, chopped
- 7 eggs
- Salt and pepper to taste
- Coconut oil for frying

Directions:

1. Preheat your oven to 375°F.
2. In the bottom of a 10-inch ovenproof frying pan, melt enough coconut oil to cover the bottom.
3. Place the broccoli and onions in the frying pan and cook until the onions are translucent.
4. Now add the squash, meat, and sun-dried tomatoes and cook gently until the squash is tender.
5. Now spread the mixture around the bottom of the frying pan evenly.
6. In a bowl, whisk together the eggs until thoroughly blended and pour them over the mixture in the frying pan.
7. Cook over medium low heat until you see the eggs firming up along the edge of the pan.
8. Place the frying pan into your preheated oven and cook for 10 to 12 minutes.
9. The frittata is done when the middle is firm.

SOUTH OF THE BORDER FRITTATA

Ingredients:

♦ 1 tablespoon coconut oil
♦ ¼ cup onion, finely chopped
♦ 1 jalapeno pepper, chopped with seeds removed
♦ 1 pound ground beef
♦ 1 cup grated, raw sweet potato
♦ 2 garlic cloves, minced
♦ 1 tablespoons chili powder
♦ 1 teaspoon ground cumin
♦ ½ cup unsweetened salsa
♦ 12 eggs
♦ Salt and pepper to taste

Directions:

1. Preheat your oven to 350°F.
2. In a large frying pan, sauté the onions and jalapeno in the coconut oil until the onions are tender.
3. Add the ground beef and cook just until it starts to brown.
4. Add the potato and garlic to the frying pan.
5. Cook until the beef is completely browned and the sweet potato is soft.
6. Add the chili powder, cumin, and salsa.
7. Stir in the spices and salsa and heat through.
8. At this point, taste the mixture and season with salt and pepper as desired.
9. Remove from heat and transfer the meat mixture to an 11 × 7 inch glass baking dish.

10. Spread the meat mixture evenly over the bottom of the glass pan.
11. In a separate mixing bowl, break open the eggs and beat together thoroughly.
12. Pour the eggs over the meat mixture in the baking dish.
13. Cover the glass pan with aluminum foil.
14. Bake in a 350°F oven for 30 minutes.
15. After 30 minutes, remove the foil and bake for an additional 10 to 15 minutes—until the eggs are set in the middle when you jiggle the pan.
16. Once firmness is achieved, remove from the oven and allow to cool briefly.
17. Cut into serving sizes and enjoy.

PALEOLITHIC QUICHE CUPS

Ingredients:

- ½ pound of meat (ground pork and turkey work well)
- 1 cup of vegetables of your choosing: chopped spinach, scallions or onions, fresh mushrooms, or bell peppers
- ⅓ cup shredded cheese (Optional: make it aged cheese)
- 5 eggs
- ¾ cup coconut or almond milk

Directions:

1. Preheat your oven to 325°F.
2. Grease a muffin tin with olive oil.
3. Cook the meat of your choice and drain if necessary.
4. Sauté the vegetables until tender.
5. Combine sautéed vegetables and cheese in a bowl and set aside.
6. Whisk together the eggs and milk and pour equal amounts of batter into each cup of prepared muffin tin.
7. Add desired amount of meat and veggie/cheese mixture to each muffin cup.
8. Bake for 20 to 25 minutes or until golden brown.
9. Briefly allow to cool.
10. Remove muffins from pan and enjoy.

TURKEY & EGGS

Ingredients:

- ½ pound ground turkey
- 3 tablespoons finely chopped onions
- 2 teaspoons coconut aminos
- ½ teaspoon cayenne pepper
- ½ teaspoon garlic powder
- 1 teaspoon salt
- 1 teaspoon black pepper
- Coconut oil or spray for frying
- 4 eggs

Directions:

1. In a large bowl, combine the turkey, onions, aminos, cayenne pepper, garlic powder, salt, and pepper.
2. Mix until all the ingredients are blended together.
3. Form this mixture into four patties.
4. Place a large skillet over medium heat and place just enough coconut oil or spray to coat the pan.
5. Place the four patties into the frying pan.
6. Cook for about 5 minutes and then turn the patties over.
7. Heat for an additional 5 minutes, until the patties have cooked thoroughly.
8. Set this pan aside or remove the patties so you can proceed with the same pan for the next step.
9. In a heated frying pan, carefully crack one egg at a time, doing your best to keep the egg in a rounded shape. This works best when your pan is hot.

10. Cover the frying pan and cook for 3 to 5 minutes—until the egg whites are no longer runny.
11. Remove the eggs when they are done and place one egg on top of a meat patty.
12. Top with salt and pepper as desired.

CHILI CREPES

Ingredients:

- ¼ cup water
- ¼ cup each of onions, mushrooms, red and green peppers. Diced for cooking
- 1 pound lean ground beef
- ½ teaspoon salt
- ¼ teaspoon garlic powder
- ½ teaspoon chili powder
- 1½ teaspoon coconut aminos
- Black pepper
- 3 tablespoons of green onions, diced to use as a garnish

Crepe

- 3 eggs
- ¼ cup coconut flour
- ½ cup almond or coconut milk
- ¼ cup water
- Dash of salt

Directions:

1. In a large heated skillet, add the water, onions, mushrooms, and red and green peppers.
2. Heat on high until onions become tender, which will take about 7 to 8 minutes.
3. Now break up the meat and combine it into the vegetable mixture.
4. Add in the salt, garlic powder, chili powder, aminos, and black pepper.
5. Continue over medium heat, stirring occasionally, until the meat is cooked through.
6. Take the beef mixture and scoop it into a bowl and set aside.

Now it's time to start your crepes.

7. Whisk all the ingredients for the crepes together in a large bowl.
8. Be sure to break up any clumps of flour as you mix ingredients together.
9. Heat a skillet on the top of your stove and grease lightly with coconut oil.
10. Pour about ¼ cup of crepe batter into your pan and swirl the batter around to evenly coat the pan.
11. Heat on medium-high heat until you begin to notice tiny bubbles forming throughout the crepe.
12. The sides of the crepe should also become golden brown in color.
13. With a soft spatula, carefully lift the crepe from the pan and place it on a plate large enough to accommodate the crepe.
14. Fill the crepe with the meat mixture by placing it down the middle of the crepe.
15. Top the meat mixture with the green onions.
16. Fold one end over the mixture and begin to roll and you tuck the sides into the middle.
17. Serve with fresh fruit.

RED PEPPER & ARUGULA OMELET

Ingredients:

- Coconut oil for frying
- 1 onion, sliced
- 1 red pepper, chopped
- 1 cup chopped arugula
- 1 tomato, chopped
- 4 eggs, beaten
- Salt and pepper to taste
- Juice from one lemon

Directions:

1. In a frying pan, place a small amount of coconut oil and turn the stove top burner up to medium heat.
2. Once the oil is heated, add the sliced onions and cook them until they become translucent.
3. Next add the chopped bell peppers and sauté them until they are slightly soft.
4. Drop in the arugula and chopped tomato and mix well.
5. Sauté the ingredients for about three minutes.
6. Pour in the scrambled eggs and continue to stir well until the eggs are cooked through.
7. Remove from the pan and place on a plate.
8. Drizzle fresh lemon juice over the top if you like.

B.B.C. FRITTATA

Ingredients:

- ♦ ½ pound bacon, cooked and crumbled (Nitrite/nitrate free is preferable)
- ♦ 1 head of broccoli, florets only
- ♦ 8 eggs
- ♦ 1½ cups coconut milk
- ♦ 1 tablespoon ghee or butter, melted
- ♦ ½ cup shredded aged cheese (optional)
- ♦ Salt and pepper to taste
- ♦ Coconut oil for frying

Directions:

1. Preheat your oven to 425°F. (This recipe requires a frying pan that can be placed in an oven.)
2. Cook bacon on the stove in a frying pan or microwave until desired crispness is achieved.
3. Cut the florets off the head of the broccoli and tenderize them in a microwave dish or on the stove in boiling water for 4 to 5 minutes.
4. In a separate bowl, whisk together the eggs, coconut milk, butter, salt, and pepper.
5. Now stir in the broccoli and crumbled bacon.
6. Pour the mixture into a frying pan that has a small amount of coconut oil melted in it.
7. Cook over medium heat until the sides of the frittata begin to firm up.
8. Remove from stove top and sprinkle the frittata with the shredded cheese.
9. Place the entire frying pan into your preheated oven.
10. Cook for 15 to 20 minutes until the center of the frittata is firm.

11. Remove from the oven and allow to rest for 5 to 10 minutes.
12. Cut into wedges and enjoy.

SAVORY BREAKFAST CASSEROLE

Ingredients:

- 6 eggs
- ¼ pound cooked meat of your choice
- ¼ cup fresh sliced mushrooms
- 3 tablespoons chopped onions
- 1 teaspoon each of salt and pepper
- ½ teaspoon garlic powder
- ½ teaspoon paprika
- ½ teaspoon dried thyme
- Aged shredded cheese for topping (optional)

Directions:

1. Preheat your oven to 350°F.
2. In a large bowl, combine all the ingredients except the cheese you will use as a topping, and mix until all the ingredients are thoroughly blended.
3. Pour mixture into a greased 8 × 8 baking dish.
4. Sprinkle the top of the batter with shredded cheese.
5. Place in preheated oven and bake for 45 minutes.
6. Slice and serve.

ZUCCHINI PORK CASSEROLE

Ingredients:

- 1 red onion, chopped
- 4 garlic cloves, minced
- 8 eggs
- 2 cups shredded pork
- 1 zucchini, peeled and shredded
- 2 tablespoons basil
- Salt and pepper to taste

Directions:

1. Preheat your oven to 350°F.
2. Sauté your onions and garlic in a frying pan over medium heat until the onions start to caramelize.
3. Turn off the heat and allow the onions to remain in the pan.
4. In a mixing bowl, combine the eggs, shredded pork, shredded zucchini, basil, salt, and pepper, and mix until thoroughly blended.
5. Add in the sautéed onions and garlic and blend well.
6. In a greased 9 × 13 inch baking pan, pour the mixture into the baking dish and distribute evenly.
7. Place the dish into the oven and bake for approximately 30 minutes. Test the center for doneness.
8. If you want the top to be browned, you can place the dish under the broiler for 4 to 5 minutes.
9. Cut and serve.

Muffins & Breads

HEARTY MORNING EGG CUPS

Ingredients:

- 1 tablespoon olive oil OR olive-oil spray
- 2 cups small, cooked, meat cubes
- 12 eggs
- Salt and pepper to taste
- ¼ cup aged shredded cheese (optional if you don't eat dairy)
- 3 tablespoons sliced chives

Directions:

1. Preheat oven to 350°F.
2. Gently wipe each muffin cup with olive oil or lightly spray the muffin cups with an olive oil spray.
3. Place a few meat cubes in the bottom of each cup.
4. Crack an egg and allow it to drop on top of the meat.
5. Continue this process until all your muffin cups are filled with an egg.
6. Season each egg cup with sea salt and pepper to your liking.
7. Top each egg with a small amount of shredded cheese and sliced chives if desired.
8. Bake for 20 minute until eggs are thoroughly cooked.
9. Remove from the muffin cups and serve warm.

CRANBERRY ALMOND BREAD

Ingredients:

- 4 eggs
- 2 medium zucchini, grated
- ½ cup almond butter
- 1 cup dried, unsweetened cranberries
- 1 cup almond meal
- 2 tablespoons raw honey
- 1½ teaspoon cinnamon
- 1½ teaspoon nutmeg
- 1 teaspoon pumpkin pie spice
- 1 teaspoon baking soda
- ¼ teaspoon sea salt
- ¼ teaspoon ground cloves
- ¾ cup chopped walnuts

Directions:

1. Preheat your oven to 350°F.
2. Prepare a 9 × 5 loaf pan with olive oil spray or apply olive oil with a paper towel.
3. Separate egg yolks from the egg whites and put each in a separate bowl.
4. Beat the egg yolks well.
5. Combine all the remaining ingredients with the egg yolks, except for the walnuts.
6. Mix all the ingredients well.

7. In a separate bowl, whip the egg whites with an electric beater until they form stiff peaks.
8. Fold in the egg whites with the egg/zucchini mixture.
9. Gently mix in the chopped walnuts.
10. Pour the batter into your greased loaf pan.
11. Bake for 60 minutes until the top is a golden brown color.
12. Test for doneness by inserting a toothpick or cake tester in the center of the bread. It is done when only crumbs appear on the toothpick or tester.
13. Allow the bread to cool for 15 to 20 minutes before removing it from the pan.
14. Slice to desired thickness and enjoy.

PUMPKIN GINGERBREAD MUFFINS

Ingredients:

- ½ cup coconut flour
- 2 teaspoons ground cinnamon
- ½ teaspoon ground nutmeg
- ½ teaspoon ground ginger powder
- ¼ teaspoon ground cloves
- ½ teaspoon baking soda
- ½ teaspoon baking powder
- ½ teaspoon salt
- 1 cup canned 100% pureed pumpkin
- 4 eggs
- 2–3 tablespoon olive or coconut oil
- ¼ cup raw honey or pure maple syrup
- 1 teaspoon pure vanilla extract
- Pumpkin seeds or walnuts, for topping

Directions:

1. Preheat oven to 400°F.
2. Lightly oil your muffin pan with coconut oil or spray.
3. In a medium-sized bowl, combine the flour, spices, soda, powder, and salt.
4. In another bowl, pour in the pumpkin puree.
5. Add the eggs one at a time, mixing well after each addition.
6. Add the olive oil, honey, and vanilla and mix until blended.

7. Combine the flour mixture into the pumpkin mixture and stir with a whisk until most lumps have disappeared.
8. Take a large spoon and place equal amounts into your prepared muffin pan, filling each muffin about ⅔ full.
9. Sprinkle the top of each muffin with a few seeds or walnuts.
10. Place muffin tins into preheated oven and bake for 18 to 20 minutes or until a tester into the middle of a muffin comes out with crumbs—not liquid batter.
11. Dump the muffins out onto a wire rack to cool.

ALMOND BANANA BREAD

Ingredients:

- 1 cup almond butter
- 1 cup shredded unsweetened coconut
- 2 medium-sized, ripe bananas
- 2 eggs
- 1 teaspoon baking powder
- 1 teaspoon baking soda
- ¼ cup 100% canned pumpkin
- 3 tablespoon unsweetened cacao powder
- 1 tablespoon raw honey, if desired

Directions:

1. Preheat your oven to 350°F.
2. In a mixing bowl, combine the almond butter, coconut, bananas, eggs, powder, and soda.
3. Be sure to mash up the bananas as best you can so they incorporate well into the batter.
4. Pour this mixture into a greased loaf pan.
5. In a separate bowl, stir together the pumpkin, cocoa powder, and honey.
6. Pour this mixture down the center of the banana batter in the loaf pan and use a knife to swirl it into the batter.
7. Place the loaf pan into a preheated oven and bake for about 35 to 40 minutes. The center should be firm when you jiggle the pan, and only crumbs should be on a toothpick or cake tester when inserted and removed.
8. Allow the bread to cool slightly before placing on a cooling rack.
9. When cooled, slice to your desired thickness.

CINNAMON SWEET BUNS

Ingredients:

- 2–3 tablespoons coconut flour
- ¼ teaspoon baking soda
- ⅛ teaspoon sea salt
- ¼ teaspoon cinnamon
- Pinch of nutmeg
- ⅛ teaspoon pure almond extract
- 1 egg
- 2 tablespoons almond or coconut milk
- 1–2 tablespoons olive or coconut oil
- 1 tablespoon raw honey
- 1–1½ cups chopped dried fruit

Directions:

1. Preheat oven to 375°F.
2. Combine coconut flour, baking soda, salt, cinnamon, and nutmeg in a small bowl.
3. Mix well.
4. Make a well in the center of the mixture.
5. Add the almond extract, egg, milk, oil, and honey into the well.
6. Stir thoroughly with a fork, eliminating as many lumps as possible.
7. Let the batter rest for a couple of minutes to allow the coconut flour to absorb the liquid.
8. Spoon the batter onto a parchment-lined baking sheet.
9. Spread out the batter and mold it into a ½-inch thick rectangle.
10. Spread dried fruit onto the top of the batter and sprinkle with cinnamon.

11. Using the edge of the parchment paper, roll up your fruit-topped batter like a cinnamon roll.
12. Bake the roll for 20 to 25 minutes, until the roll is golden brown.
13. Remove from oven and allow to cool briefly.
14. Slice into desired thickness and enjoy.

BANANA ALMOND MUFFINS

Ingredients:

- ½ cup coconut flour
- ¼ cup almond meal
- ½ teaspoon baking powder
- ¼ teaspoon baking soda
- ⅓ cup raw honey
- Pinch of sea salt
- 4 eggs
- 1 heaping tablespoon almond butter
- 2 very ripe bananas, mashed
- 1 teaspoon pure vanilla extract
- 1 teaspoon olive or coconut oil

Directions:

1. In a mixing bowl, combine the flour, almond meal, baking powder, baking soda, honey, and salt.
2. In a different bowl, combine the eggs, almond butter, bananas, vanilla, and oil.
3. Slowly add the dry ingredients into the bowl with the wet ingredients and stir until the batter looks uniform in consistency.
4. Evenly divide the batter into your lightly greased muffin tin pan.
5. Bake in a 375°F oven for 20 to 25 minutes.
6. Remove the muffins from the oven when cooked and allow to cool for a few minutes in the pan.
7. Dump the muffins onto a cooling rack and eat when ready.

Pancakes & Waffles

COCONUT FLOUR PANCAKES

Ingredients:

- 3 eggs, room temperature
- 1 teaspoon pure vanilla extract
- ½ cup coconut milk
- ¼ teaspoon sea salt
- ½ teaspoon baking soda
- ⅓ cup coconut flour

Directions:

1. In a bowl and using a hand mixer, whip the eggs until foamy. Do this for approximately two minutes
2. Add the vanilla and milk and mix until thoroughly blended
3. In a separate bowl, combine the salt, soda, and flour and mix thoroughly.
4. Pour the flour mixture into the eggs and mix completely.
5. Lightly oil griddle with coconut oil and place over medium heat.
6. Pour a small amount of batter onto heated griddle and spread out some with the back of your spoon.
7. Cook until bubbles begin to appear in the pancake and along the sides.
8. Gently flip the pancake over and cook until browned.
9. Top with your favorite topping.

FREEDOM WAFFLES

Ingredients:

- 2 large eggs
- ¼ cup almond or coconut milk
- 1½ cup almond flour
- 1 teaspoon sea salt
- 1 teaspoon baking soda
- Dash of cinnamon

Directions:

1. Preheat your waffle iron to your desired setting.
2. Whisk eggs and milk together until foamy.
3. Combine all the remaining dry ingredients together in a separate bowl and mix thoroughly.
4. Add the egg/milk mixture into the bowl with the combined dry ingredients and mix until smooth.
5. Put ¼ cup of batter into the preheated waffle iron.
6. Cook until golden brown and then remove.
7. Top with fresh fruit of your choice and/or almond butter.
8. Yum!

NUTTY PANCAKES

Ingredients:

- 1 cup chestnut flour
- ½ cup almond meal
- ⅔ cup coconut or almond milk
- 1 tablespoon raw honey (optional)
- 2 egg whites
- Coconut oil for frying

Directions:

1. Combine the flour, almond meal, milk, and honey in a bowl and mix well.
2. In a separate bowl, beat the egg whites until stiff peaks form.
3. Gently fold the egg whites into the batter.
4. Place a small amount of coconut oil in a frying pan and heat over medium heat.
5. Once heated, place about two tablespoons of batter into the frying pan, or more if you like bigger pancakes.
6. Allow small bubbles to form and sides to harden slightly, about 2 to 3 minutes, then flip the pancake.
7. Once the second side is golden brown, remove from the frying pan.
8. Serve warm and top with your favorite topping, such as maple syrup and berries.

FLUFFY COCONUT PANCAKES

Ingredients:

- 4 eggs at room temperature
- 1 cup coconut milk
- 2 teaspoon pure vanilla extract
- 1 tablespoon raw honey (optional)
- ½ cup coconut flour
- 1 teaspoon baking soda
- ½ teaspoon sea salt
- Coconut oil for frying

Directions:

1. In a bowl, whisk the eggs together well until foamy.
2. Pour in the milk, vanilla, and honey into the eggs and mix well.
3. In a separate bowl, combine flour, soda, and salt and mix well.
4. Place a frying pan or griddle over medium heat with enough coconut oil to just cover the bottom.
5. Once the oil is heated, pour or spoon batter to form your pancake.
6. Cook until the edges of the pancake start to dry and harden and bubbles form throughout the pancake.
7. Flip the pancake and cook until golden brown.
8. Top your pancake with your favorite topping, like berries and maple syrup.

SWEET POTATO LATKES

Ingredients:

- 5 cups grated sweet potato
- 2 eggs
- 2 tablespoons onions, minced
- 1 teaspoon cinnamon
- Salt and pepper to taste
- Coconut oil for frying

Directions:

1. Mix all the ingredients together in a large mixing bowl.
2. Heat a griddle or frying pan over medium heat and melt a spoonful of coconut oil.
3. Take a small amount of the potato mixture and drop it onto the hot griddle or skillet and form little cakes.
4. Cook for 3 to 5 minutes on each side, cooking until each side is golden brown and heated all the way through.
5. Top the latkes with favorites like fried eggs and bacon if you wish.

APPLE CINNAMON PANCAKES

Ingredients:

- ½ cup almond meal
- ½ cup green apple, grated
- 4 egg whites
- ¼ cup raw honey or coconut sugar
- ¼ cup almond milk, coconut milk, or water
- 1 tablespoon fresh lemon juice
- ½ teaspoon baking soda
- ¼ teaspoon cinnamon
- ¼ teaspoon salt

Directions:

1. In a large bowl, combine all ingredients until blended and the consistency of a pourable batter.
2. Set the batter aside while you heat your frying pan on the stove top.
3. Spray your frying pan with cooking spray or coconut oil.
4. Spoon ¼ cup of the pancake batter into the frying pan and cook on medium-high for 5 minutes on each side.
5. Remove from the pan and eat!

Grainless Cereals

COCONUT BLACKBERRY BARS

Ingredients:

- 1 cup almond flour
- ½ cup shredded unsweetened coconut
- 1 teaspoon cinnamon
- 1 teaspoon baking powder
- ½ teaspoon baking soda
- ½ teaspoon sea salt
- ¼ cup raw honey
- 2 ripe bananas, mashed
- 2 eggs
- 2 tablespoons melted coconut oil or olive oil
- 1 teaspoon pure vanilla extract
- ¾ cup almond or coconut milk
- 1 cup blackberries, fresh or thawed

Directions:

1. Preheat oven to 350°F.
2. Prepare an 8 × 8 baking pan with coconut spray or olive oil spray and set aside.
3. Using a large bowl, mix together the flour, shredded coconut, cinnamon, baking powder and soda, and salt.
4. Add your sweetener to this mixture and blend.

5. Now add in the bananas, eggs, oil, vanilla, and ¼ cup of almond milk.
6. Mix until all the ingredients are moist.
7. Be sure the batter has the consistency of a cookie batter so add the necessary amount of almond milk to achieve this.
8. Gently fold in the blackberries, being careful not to tear them up too much.
9. Spoon the batter into the greased pan.
10. Bake for approximately 40 minutes or until the batter is golden brown at the sides.
11. Remove pan from the oven and cool.

CHOCOLATE GRANOLA CRUNCH

Ingredients:

- ½ cup raw sunflower seeds
- ½ cup raw pumpkin seeds
- 1 cup almond meal
- 1 cup shredded unsweetened coconut
- 2 cups raw almonds, slivered or chopped
- 2 tablespoons unsweetened cacao powder
- Pinch of ground cinnamon
- ½ cup coconut oil
- ½ cup raw honey
- 1 teaspoon pure vanilla extract

Directions:

1. Preheat your oven to 325°F.
2. Take a large mixing bowl and combine the sunflower seeds, pumpkin seeds, almond meal, coconut, almonds, cacao powder, and cinnamon.
3. In a microwave-safe bowl, combine the remaining ingredients of oil, honey, and vanilla.
4. Place the bowl of wet ingredients into the microwave and microwave on high for 20 to 30 seconds to warm. This will allow your mixture to handle better.
5. Place the wet ingredients into the dry ingredients and stir well. Be sure everything is evenly coated.
6. Place the mixture onto a foil-lined cookie sheet or one that has been prepared with coconut spray or olive oil.

7. Spread evenly over the cookie sheet.
8. Place the cookie sheet into the oven.
9. Bake in the oven for 25 to 30 minutes, being careful that the mixture doesn't burn. (You may want to stir it once during the process so it cooks evenly.)
10. Now remove the cookie sheet from the oven and allow to cool. You will find this mixture gets crunchy as it gets colder.
11. This recipe can be used in place of a grain cereal by putting into a bowl with some milk or eaten plain.

CRANBERRY DOUBLE NUT GRANOLA

Ingredients:

- 1 cup toasted pecans
- 1 cup toasted sliced almonds
- 1 cup dried, unsweetened cranberries
- ¼ teaspoon ground cinnamon
- Salt to taste

Directions:

1. Blend all the ingredients in a bowl.
2. Eat plain as a snack or with almond or coconut milk.

Smoothies & More

BANANA BERRY SMOOTHIE

Ingredients:

- 1 ripe banana
- ½ cup frozen berries
- 1 cup coconut water
- Thumbnail-sized piece of fresh ginger
- 1 teaspoon cinnamon
- 1 tablespoon raw honey
- 2 cups ice

Directions:

1. Place all the ingredients into a blender.
2. Process on high until a smooth consistency is achieved.
3. Pour into a large glass and enjoy the energy boost.

BERRY NUTTY BREAKFAST SMOOTHIE

Ingredients:

- 1 cup almond milk, coconut milk, or water
- ½ cup frozen berries
- ¼ cup walnuts
- 1 tablespoon raw honey
- 1 teaspoon cinnamon
- 1 cup ice

Directions:

1. Place all the ingredients into a blender.
2. Process on high until a smooth consistency is achieved.
3. Pour into a large glass and enjoy the energy boost.

BREAKFAST SAUSAGE

Ingredients:

- 2 pounds ground beef
- 1 pound ground pork
- 2 teaspoons fresh thyme, chopped
- 2 teaspoons fresh sage, chopped
- 1 teaspoon fresh rosemary, chopped
- 2 teaspoons sea salt
- 1½ teaspoons black pepper
- 1 teaspoon fresh grated nutmeg
- ½ teaspoon cayenne

Directions:

1. Begin by combining all of your ingredients in a large mixing bowl.
2. Form meat mixture into little round balls or links, 1 to 2 inches in diameter.
3. Heat a frying pan or skillet on the stove over a medium setting using a small amount of coconut oil in the bottom.
4. Carefully place the meat rounds in the pan and cook for 10 to 15 minutes—until they are browned and cooked through.
5. Remove the meat from the pan and drain any excess oil or grease.

LUNCHES

Salads

HEARTY SAUTÉED PEACH SALAD

Ingredients:

- 3 cups fresh romaine lettuce, washed
- ½ cup grated carrots
- ¾ cup sliced peaches
- 1 cup shredded chicken
- 2 tablespoons coconut oil
- 1 teaspoon cinnamon
- 1 teaspoon nutmeg

Directions:

1. Sauté sliced fresh peaches. Sauté in virgin coconut oil until tender and set aside.
2. Mix peaches, chicken, cinnamon, and nutmeg together.
3. Top romaine with peaches and add an oil and vinegar dressing of your choice.

BROCCOLI & BACON SALAD

If you allow yourself to eat bacon on occasion, you will truly enjoy the taste of this salad.

Ingredients:

- 8 ounces plain Greek yogurt or kefir (if you eat dairy)
- 1 egg
- 2 tablespoons vinegar
- 2 tablespoons raw honey
- 1 tablespoon olive or coconut oil
- 1 tablespoon mustard
- ¼ teaspoon sea salt
- ⅛ teaspoon garlic powder
- ⅛ teaspoon pepper
- 6 cups fresh broccoli, cut into bite-size pieces
- ⅓ cup raisins (optional)
- 2 tablespoons chopped onions
- ½ pound bacon, cooked and crumbled

Directions:

1. Blend first nine ingredients in blender until smooth.
2. In large mixing bowl, combine broccoli, raisins, onions, and bacon.
3. Pour sauce over mixture, then chill at least four hours.

GRILLED TACO SALAD

Ingredients:

- 4 tablespoons olive or coconut oil
- 2 hearts of romaine lettuce, cut into quarters
- 1 onion, cut into chunks
- 1 green pepper, cut into chunks
- 2 tomatoes, cut into chunks
- 2 avocados, peeled, pitted, and cut in half
- 1 pound skirt steak
- ½ teaspoon cumin
- ¼ teaspoon paprika
- ¼ teaspoon chili powder
- ¼ teaspoon salt

Directions:

1. Turn your grill on to medium heat.
2. Take a large bowl and place the romaine quarters, onion, green pepper, tomatoes, and avocados into it.
3. Drizzle 2 tablespoons of olive oil over the vegetables and toss to coat.
4. Place the vegetables, including the romaine, into a grill basket or on skewers.
5. In a small bowl, mix the other 2 tablespoons of oil with the cumin, paprika, chili powder, and salt.
6. Coat the steak with the spice mixture.
7. Place the steak onto the grill, along with the vegetables.
8. Close the lid and grill for 4 minutes.
9. After 4 minutes, flip the steak and grill basket to the other side.

10. Close the lid and grill for 4 more minutes.
11. After the steak is done to your liking, slice it and cut the romaine into bite-sized chunks.
12. Toss with the vegetables and add salt and pepper to taste.

FRUITY SALAD WITH CHICKEN

Ingredients:

- 12 ounces of canned white chicken
- 2 celery stalks, finely chopped
- ¼ cup chopped red onion
- ¼ cup homemade Paleolithic mayonnaise
- ½ cup dried cranberries

Directions:

1. In a medium-sized bowl, put the chicken, celery, onion, mayo, and cranberries.
2. Mix well.
3. Enjoy as a wrap using lettuce leaves, or as a dip with carrot chips and celery.

How to Make Paleolithic Mayonnaise

Ingredients:

- 2 tablespoons fresh-squeezed lemon juice
- 2 large eggs
- 1 teaspoon dry mustard
- Salt to taste. Start with 1 teaspoon.
- ¼ teaspoon cayenne pepper (optional)
- 2 cups olive oil

Directions:

1. In a blender, add the lemon juice, eggs, dry mustard, salt, and cayenne (if using).
2. Pulse for a few seconds until the mixture becomes frothy.
3. Turn your blender on a low setting and allow it to keep running.
4. Slowly add the oil—almost a drop at a time—to the mixture until it begins to emulsify.
5. Keep adding the oil slowly until it is all blended in.
6. Add salt to taste.
7. Store in a container in your refrigerator.

ASIAN LOBSTER SALAD

Ingredients:

- 1 pound cooked lobster meat
- 2 cups thinly sliced Napa cabbage
- ½ red bell pepper, thinly sliced
- 8-ounce can of water chestnuts, drained
- ½ cup fresh parsley, chopped
- ¼ cup slivered almonds, toasted

Dressing:

- 2 tablespoons chicken broth
- 2 tablespoons coconut aminos
- 1 tablespoon olive oil
- 1 teaspoon sesame oil
- 1 teaspoon fresh ginger, grated

Directions:

1. Cut lobster meat into 1-inch pieces.
2. Mix with cabbage, bell pepper, water chestnuts, parsley, and almonds.
3. In a small bowl, whisk together the vinegar, aminos, olive oil, sesame oil, and ginger.
4. Pour dressing over salad.
5. Toss gently to coat.

WARM SHRIMP SALAD

Ingredients:

- ♦ Juice of 3 lemons
- ♦ 3 tablespoons raw honey
- ♦ 1 teaspoon minced garlic
- ♦ Salt & pepper to taste
- ♦ 2 tablespoons olive oil
- ♦ ½ pound large raw shrimp, peeled and cleaned
- ♦ ¼ teaspoon fresh ginger, finely grated
- ♦ ½ cup snap peas, diced
- ♦ 2 medium sized zucchini, diced
- ♦ ½ cup broccoli sprouts
- ♦ 2 tablespoons toasted sesame seeds (optional)

Directions:

1. In a small bowl, whisk together the lemon juice, honey, garlic, salt, and pepper.
2. Pour half of the mixture over the shrimp, allowing it to marinate for a few minutes.
3. Heat the olive oil in a large skillet over medium-high heat.
4. Once hot, add the shrimp to the skillet and sauté until pink and cooked through.
5. In a medium bowl, combine the ginger, snap peas, zucchini, and broccoli sprouts.
6. Toss the warm, cooked shrimp into the bowl.
7. Toss with remaining half of the lemon juice mixture and sesame seeds.
8. Serve immediately.

POACHED EGG SALAD

Ingredients:

- 4 eggs
- 3 tablespoons lemon juice
- 2 teaspoons Dijon mustard
- ¾ teaspoon salt
- ½ teaspoon pepper
- ½ cup olive or coconut oil
- 4 ounces lean sausage
- 6 cups mixed greens
- 4 ounces aged cheddar cheese, shredded (optional)

Directions:

1. Poach eggs in an egg poacher, saucepan, or microwave.
2. Cook until the egg whites are set but the yolks are still runny—about 4 minutes in an egg poacher or 2 minutes in the microwave.
3. To make the dressing, combine the lemon juice, mustard, salt, and pepper in a blender.
4. Pour into a medium bowl and slowly whisk in the olive oil until the dressing thickens.
5. Set aside.
6. Place a frying pan over medium heat and sauté the beef until browned.
7. Toss the mixed greens with the dressing.
8. Sprinkle with the ground beef and shredded cheese.
9. Finally, place one egg on top of each serving of salad.

Soups

CABBAGE AND BEEF SOUP

Ingredients:

- ½ pound stewing beef
- 3 quarts water
- 2 bay leaves
- 1 small head of cabbage
- 4 large carrots
- 4 stalks of celery
- 1 large onion
- 15-ounce can diced tomatoes
- 8 ounces 100% tomato juice

Directions:

1. Place the beef into a large pot and fill with 3 quarts of water.
2. Add the bay leaves.
3. Cover the pot and simmer for 3 hours to make sure the beef is tender.
4. Chop the cabbage, carrots, celery, and onion.
5. Now add the vegetables to the pot with the beef. Cook for additional 30 minutes.
6. Remove the bay leaves and add the tomatoes and the tomato juice.
7. Bring to a boil again and serve.

SWEET POTATO SOUP

Ingredients:

- 1 tablespoon coconut flour
- 1 tablespoon coconut oil
- 1½ cups chicken broth
- 1½ cups cooked, cubed sweet potatoes
- ¼ teaspoon ground ginger (or fresh, to taste)
- ⅛ teaspoon ground cinnamon
- ⅛ teaspoon ground nutmeg
- 1 cup coconut or almond milk
- Salt and pepper to taste

Directions:

1. In a saucepan over medium-low heat, cook the coconut flour and coconut oil, stirring constantly until the mixture turns a light caramel color.
2. Add the chicken broth and bring it to a boil.
3. Turn the heat down to low and then stir in the sweet potatoes, ginger, cinnamon, and nutmeg.
4. Cook on low for 5 more minutes and blend thoroughly.
5. Remove from the pot and place the mixture into a blender.
6. Puree the soup.
7. Now return to the saucepan.
8. Now add the coconut or almond milk and gently reheat the soup.
9. Season with salt and pepper and serve.

EASY VEGETABLE SOUP

Ingredients:

♦ 2 tablespoons coconut oil

♦ ¼ cup diced onion

♦ 1 cup thinly sliced carrots

♦ 1 cup thinly sliced zucchini

♦ 2 teaspoons fresh parsley

♦ ¼ teaspoon thyme

♦ ⅛ teaspoon pepper

♦ 2 cups water

Directions:

1. In a medium saucepan, heat up the coconut oil.
2. Once heated, add the onion and cook until it is translucent.
3. Add the carrots, zucchini, parsley, thyme, and pepper to the saucepan.
4. Cover and cook over low heat until the vegetables are tender—approximately 10 minutes.
5. Add the water and bring to a boil.
6. Reduce the heat to medium and cook until vegetables are soft—approximately 20 minutes. Once you've finished cooking the vegetables, remove the pot from the heat and allow it to cool slightly.
7. Remove ½ cup of soup from the pan and put it aside.
8. Pour the remaining soup into a blender and process at low speed until you've reached a smooth consistency.

9. Combine the pureed mixture and the reserved soup into a saucepan and cook, stirring constantly until it is hot.

10. Serve and enjoy.

CHICKEN CHOWDER

Ingredients:

- 4 cups chicken, cubed
- 6 cups water
- 1 large chopped onion, divided in half
- 2 stalks celery, chopped, divided in half
- 1 cup chopped carrot, divided in half
- 6 large cloves garlic, finely chopped, divided in half
- ¼ cup chopped parsley, divided in half
- ½ teaspoon black pepper—more if desired
- 3 cups chicken stock
- 2 tablespoons olive or coconut oil
- 2 tablespoons coconut flour
- ½ cup coconut or almond milk
- Salt to your liking

Directions:

1. Place the chicken, water, half of the onion, half of the celery, half of the carrot, half of the garlic, parsley, and black pepper in a small stockpot.
2. Bring the mixture to a boil.
3. Now reduce the heat, cover and let simmer for 45 minutes to 1 hour.
4. Strain the broth into another pot through a colander.
5. Discard the cooked vegetables.
6. Add the chicken stock to the pot and set aside.
7. In the large stockpot, heat the oil over medium heat.

8. Add the flour and the remaining onion, celery, carrot, garlic, and parsley and stir constantly until the onions are fragrant and translucent—approximately 5 to 6 minutes.
9. Whisking constantly, add the flour and cook for about 1 minute.
10. Now whisk in the chicken broth, making sure to stir constantly to avoid any clumping.
11. Bring the mixture to a boil and cook until tender—approximately 8 minutes more.
12. Add the cooked chicken and coconut or almond milk and heat until just warmed.
13. Serve at desired temperature with additional salt and pepper to taste.

LOBSTER BISQUE PALEOLITHIC STYLE

Ingredients:

♦ 4 tablespoons butter or ghee

♦ 2 tablespoons scallions, diced

♦ 1 stalk celery, chopped

♦ 4 tablespoons coconut flour

♦ 2 cups PLUS 2 tablespoons coconut milk

♦ 1 tablespoon tomato paste

♦ 2 teaspoons paprika

♦ 1 teaspoon Old Bay Seasoning

♦ ⅛ teaspoon cayenne pepper

♦ 2–3 tablespoons chicken broth

♦ 10 ounces cooked, coarsely chopped lobster meat, drained well

♦ Salt and pepper to taste

Directions:

1. Melt butter in a saucepan over medium-low heat.
2. Add the scallions and celery and cook for about 3 minutes, until the vegetables begin to soften.
3. Add the coconut flour and blend into the vegetables.
4. Cook over medium heat for about 3 minutes, stirring frequently.
5. Slowly pour the coconut milk into the vegetable mixture and stir until blended.
6. Now stir in the tomato paste.
7. Cook over medium-low heat for about 5 minutes or until the bisque begins to thicken.

8. Add the paprika, Old Bay Seasoning, cayenne, and sherry.
9. Stir to blend.
10. Add the cooked lobster meat.
11. Salt and pepper to taste.
12. Simmer the bisque over low heat for about 5 more minutes, until heated through.
13. Do not boil!
14. Enjoy!

FAST & FRESH TOMATO BASIL SOUP

Ingredients:

- 3 large tomatoes, peeled and chopped
- 1 onion, chopped
- 4 garlic cloves, minced
- ½ teaspoon oregano
- ⅛ teaspoon marjoram
- ¼ cup fresh basil, coarsely chopped
- 2 cups chicken stock
- Salt and pepper to taste

Directions:

1. Place prepared tomatoes, onions, garlic, oregano, marjoram, and basil into a medium-sized saucepan. Add the chicken stock and bring to a boil.
2. Reduce the heat and simmer for approximately 20 minutes.
3. Cool for 10 minutes.
4. Pour the soup into a blender in small batches and run on high for a smooth consistency.
5. Repeat for each batch.
6. Each time, pour the soup back into another saucepan and reheat briefly before serving.
7. Garnish with fresh basil if desired.

QUICK CHICKEN & VEGGIE SOUP

Ingredients:

- 1 rotisserie chicken, meat removed and shredded
- 2 ribs of celery, chopped
- ½ red onion, finely chopped
- 4 large carrots, thinly sliced
- ½ large butternut squash, peeled and cubed
- 2 teaspoons minced garlic
- 1 teaspoon basil
- 1 teaspoon oregano
- 1 tablespoon lemon juice
- Salt and pepper, to taste
- Fresh cold water
- A few sprigs of freshly chopped parsley

Directions:

1. Add shredded chicken, celery, onion, carrots, squash, garlic, basil, oregano, lemon juice, salt, and pepper to a large pot on the stove.
2. Pour fresh cold water over the chicken and veggies until submerged.
3. Place the lid on the pot and cook on high until the squash begins to soften—approximately 20 minutes.
4. Stir and serve with a sprinkling of fresh chopped parsley.

Wraps

LETTUCE WRAPS

Ingredients:

- ◆ 1 avocado
- ◆ 1 chicken breast, cooked and cubed
- ◆ 2 tomatoes, chopped
- ◆ ¼ onion, chopped
- ◆ ½ bell pepper, chopped
- ◆ 1 clove garlic, minced
- ◆ 1 sprig fresh cilantro, minced
- ◆ Juice from 1 lime
- ◆ 4 large lettuce leaves

Directions:

1. Mash the avocado until it has a smooth texture that is spreadable.
2. To the avocado, add the chicken, tomatoes, onion, bell pepper, garlic, cilantro, and lime juice.
3. Mix well.
4. Place your desired amount of the mixture onto each lettuce leaf and wrap it up like a burrito.

CHICKEN FAJITAS

Ingredients:

- 3 pounds chicken breasts, cut into strips
- 3 bell peppers
- 3 onions, sliced
- 2 tablespoons oregano
- 2 tablespoons chili powder
- 2 tablespoons cumin
- 2 tablespoons coriander
- 6 garlic cloves, chopped
- Juice of 5 lemons
- 4 tablespoons coconut oil
- Butter lettuce leaves for the fajitas
- Favorite toppings

Directions:

1. In a large bowl, combine the chicken, bell peppers, onions, oregano, chili powder, cumin, coriander, garlic, and lemon juice into a bowl and mix well.
2. Allow the mixture to marinate in the refrigerator for 4 hours.
3. When you are ready to cook, place the coconut oil into a large skillet and melt over medium heat.
4. Cook the entire mixture until the chicken is cooked through and the onion and bell pepper are soft.
5. Remove the mixture from the heat and place into a large bowl.
6. Now place desired amount of mixture into a lettuce leaf, top with your favorite toppings, and wrap.
7. Enjoy.

NO MAYO EGG SALAD WRAP

Ingredients:

- 8 hard-boiled eggs
- 1 avocado, peeled with pit removed
- ½ teaspoon dry mustard
- 2 tablespoons apple cider vinegar
- ½ teaspoon sea salt
- Whole lettuce leaves (romaine and butter lettuce work well)

Directions:

1. Take your hard-boiled eggs and separate the yolks from the whites.
2. Place the yolks, avocado, dry mustard, vinegar and salt in a large bowl and mash until smooth.
3. Take the egg whites and chop them.
4. Now fold the egg whites and the salt into the mashed mixture.
5. Place desired amount into the lettuce leaves.
6. Serve immediately.

SPICY TUNA SALAD WRAP

Ingredients:

- 24 ounces canned tuna
- 1 tablespoon Paleolithic mayo
- ⅓ cup chopped and seeded jalapeno pepper
- ⅓ teaspoon onion powder
- ⅓ cup onion
- ½ teaspoon salt
- ¼ cup salsa
- 8-ounce can tomato paste

Directions:
1. Combine all the ingredients in a medium bowl and mix well.
2. Enjoy this salad mixture wrapped in lettuce leaves.

STEAK & SALSA WRAP

Ingredients:

- 1 serving of cooked skirt steak
- 1 tomato, chopped
- 1 avocado, peeled, pitted and cubed
- 1 teaspoon sea salt
- Juice from ½ lime
- 1 tablespoon apple cider vinegar
- 1 tablespoon olive or coconut oil
- Romaine or leafy lettuce for wraps
- Favorite salsa

Directions:

1. Place your lettuce leaf on a plate and place the skirt steak on top.
2. Put the tomato and avocado into a bowl.
3. In a small separate bowl, combine the salt, lime juice, vinegar, and oil until mixed well.
4. Pour the liquid mixture over the tomato and avocado and mix gently.
5. Top the steak with the mixture and add your favorite salsa.

ASIAN LETTUCE WRAPS

Ingredients:

- ♦ 1 tablespoon macadamia nut oil
- ♦ 3 garlic cloves, minced
- ♦ ½ red onion, chopped
- ♦ 1½ teaspoon ginger, minced
- ♦ 1 pound ground beef
- ♦ 1 tablespoon coconut aminos
- ♦ Chopped zucchini, tomatoes, shredded carrots, sliced mushrooms (optional)
- ♦ Lettuce leaves or raw cabbage leaves for the wraps
- ♦ Cilantro to garnish

Directions:

1. In a large frying pan, put the oil and heat over a medium setting.
2. Once heated, add the onion and cook until translucent.
3. Add the garlic and ginger and cook for another minute or two.
4. Add the ground beef and cook until browned.
5. Once browned, add the aminos and stir to blend.
6. Place any chopped vegetables you would like to add into the pan and cook for a few minutes.
7. Remove from the heat and place desired amount onto a lettuce or cabbage leaf.
8. Garnish with nuts, cilantro, etc. and wrap.

BASIC PALEOLITHIC WRAPS

Ingredients:

- 2 eggs
- 1 tablespoon coconut flour
- 3 tablespoons olive or coconut oil
- Salt to taste
- 3 tablespoons water

Directions:

1. Begin by whisking the eggs really well in a small bowl.
2. Process the coconut flour through a sifter.
3. Now add the flour to the whipped eggs, along with the olive oil and salt.
4. Mix well and whisk the mixture for one minute.
5. The mixture should be pourable like a pancake batter. If too thick to pour, add one tablespoon of water at a time until desired consistency is reached.
6. Heat a large frying pan with enough olive oil to cover the bottom.
7. Once the oil is heated, pour enough batter into the pan to make the size wrap you want.
8. Cook on medium heat for 3 to 4 minutes.
9. Flip to the other side and brown.
10. Fill with your favorite filling.

Quick Bites

SCALLOPS & SAUTÉED VEGGIES

Ingredients:

♦ ½ red onion, thinly sliced
♦ 6 slices of thick bacon
♦ 3 garlic cloves, minced
♦ 1 pound fresh snap peas
♦ 3 tablespoons flat leaf parsley, finely diced
♦ Juice from ½ a lemon
♦ ½ teaspoon dried thyme
♦ Salt and pepper to taste
♦ 2 tablespoons coconut oil
♦ 1 pound sea scallops, defrosted
♦ ½ cup chicken broth

Directions:

1. In a frying pan, sauté the onions and bacon for 4 minutes.
2. Add the garlic and snap peas and sauté for another 2 minutes.
3. Add the parsley, lemon juice, thyme, salt, and pepper and cook for another minute.
4. Remove the veggie mixture from the pan and set aside.
5. Add the coconut oil to the skillet and heat over medium high heat.

6. Make sure your scallops are entirely defrosted and patted dry with paper towels.
7. Sprinkle the scallops with a bit of salt and pepper and sear the scallops for 1 minute on each side (they should be nice and brown).
8. Add the veggie mixture on top of the scallops, pour the chicken broth on top and gently stir.
9. Bring to a boil and simmer for another minute or two. The scallops should be tender and cooked all the way through. Do not overcook scallops or they will turn rubbery.

CHICKEN SALAD-STUFFED TOMATOES

Ingredients:

♦ 6 large tomatoes

♦ 18 ounces of canned chicken, drained

♦ 1 cup flat-leaf parsley leaves, chopped

♦ Zest of 1 lemon

♦ ¼ cup fresh lemon juice

♦ 1 tablespoon olive or coconut oil

♦ ¼ teaspoon black pepper

Directions:

1. Begin by hollowing out each tomato. Remove the stem end and scoop out the seeds and pulp, being careful not to pierce the skin.
2. Add the canned chicken, parsley, lemon zest, juice, oil, and pepper to a bowl and mix thoroughly.
3. Carefully spoon the mixture into the hollowed-out tomatoes.
4. Yummy!

EGGPLANT BRUSCHETTA

Ingredients:

- 7 ripe plum tomatoes
- 2 teaspoons apple cider vinegar
- 1 large eggplant
- 2 large eggs
- 2 cloves garlic, minced
- 8 fresh basil leaves, chopped
- 1 teaspoon paprika
- 1 teaspoon garlic powder
- ½ teaspoon sea salt
- ½ teaspoon black pepper
- ½ teaspoon dried thyme
- 1 teaspoon chipotle powder (optional)
- 1 cup almond flour
- 1 tablespoon olive or coconut oil

Directions:

1. Preheat oven to 375°F.
2. Grease a baking sheet or pizza pan with olive oil.
3. Parboil the tomatoes for one minute in boiling water that has just been removed from the burner.
4. Drain.
5. Using a sharp small knife, remove the skins of the tomatoes.
6. Once the tomatoes are peeled, cut them in halves or quarters and remove the seeds and juice from their centers.

7. Also cut out and discard the stem area.
8. In a separate bowl, mix the tomatoes with the vinegar and set aside.
9. Slice the eggplant into 8 round slices, each about ½ inch thick.
10. Trim the skin, maintaining the round shape of the slices.
11. In a small bowl, whisk the eggs.
12. Mix dry ingredients and almond flour together and set aside in a separate small bowl.
13. Dip the eggplant slices one at a time into the egg and then into the almond flour.
14. One by one, place the coated slices in a single layer on the prepared baking sheet or pizza pan greased with the olive oil.
15. Top the slices with the tomato topping.
16. Bake in the preheated oven approximately 15 minutes.
17. Now change the oven setting to broil and continue cooking 3 to 5 minutes.
18. Check the slices frequently while broiling to avoid burning.

BALTIMORE CRAB CAKES

Ingredients:

- 1 pound crab meat
- 2 tablespoons coconut flour
  (or enough to make the mixture stick together)
- 1 egg
- ¼ cup minced fresh parsley
- 1 teaspoon crushed garlic
- ¼ cup Paleolithic mayo
- 2 tablespoons spicy mustard
- Salt and pepper to taste
- ⅛ teaspoon of chipotle powder
- 3–4 tablespoons coconut oil

Directions:

1. If using the canned crab, make sure to crumble the crab with your hands into a large mixing bowl and pick out any shells you might find.
2. Mix the crab with the coconut flour, egg, parsley, garlic, mayo, mustard, salt, pepper, and chipotle powder.
3. In a large skillet, heat the coconut oil over medium heat for about 1 minute.
4. Form the crab cake mixture into palm-sized patties and fry for 2 to 3 minutes on each side or until they are golden brown.

CRABBY MUSHROOMS

Ingredients:

- 10-ounce package frozen spinach, thawed
- 1½ pounds portabella mushrooms
- 2 tablespoons coconut oil
- ¼ cup onions, chopped
- 2 garlic cloves, minced
- ¼ cup chicken broth
- 1 tablespoon lemon juice
- ½ teaspoon dried basil
- ¼ teaspoon ground ginger
- ½ teaspoon dried oregano
- 12 ounces cooked crabmeat

Directions:

1. Preheat your oven to 425°F.
2. Begin by thawing spinach and draining the excess liquid.
3. Remove the stems and some of the inside flesh of the mushroom with a spoon.
4. Chop some of the stems to make enough for 2 cups.
5. In a large skillet, heat up the coconut oil over medium heat.
6. Once heated, add the chopped mushroom stems, onion, garlic, chicken broth, and lemon juice.
7. Cook until the onion is tender.
8. Now add the spinach and cook until the liquid is evaporated.
9. Stir in the basil, ginger, and oregano into the spinach.

10. Now add the crabmeat and mix gently.
11. Spoon the crab mixture into the mushroom tops.
12. Place the stuffed mushroom tops into a lightly greased baking dish.
13. Bake for 10 to 15 minutes, until the mushrooms are tender.
14. Remove when finished and serve.

APPLE COLESLAW

Ingredients:

- 2 cups packaged coleslaw mix (bag of chopped cabbage found in the produce section) OR shred your own cabbage
- 2 unpeeled tart apples, chopped
- ½ cup finely chopped celery
- ½ cup apple cider vinegar
- 2 tablespoons raw honey (optional)
- 1 tablespoon olive or coconut oil

Directions:

1. In a bowl, combine the coleslaw mix, apples, and celery.
2. In a separate, smaller bowl, whisk together the vinegar, honey, and oil.
3. Now pour the dressing over the coleslaw and toss together to coat the slaw.
4. Enjoy.

APRICOT AND COCONUT NUT BARS

Ingredients:

- 1 cup slivered almonds
- 1 cup pecans
- ½ cup almond flour
- ½ cup coconut oil
- ½ cup almond butter
- ¼ cup raw honey
- 2 teaspoons pure vanilla extract
- ½ teaspoon sea salt
- 1 cup of dried apricots, chopped into small pieces
- ¼–½ cup of shredded unsweetened coconut
- Parchment paper

Directions:

1. Place the slivered almonds and pecans on a cookie sheet and toast in a 350-degree oven for 8 to 10 minutes.
2. Now place the toasted nuts into a food processor and pulse until they are coarse.
3. Remove from the food processor and place in a medium bowl along with the almond flour and mix together.
4. In a microwaveable bowl, warm the coconut oil and the almond butter for about 20 seconds in the microwave until it has a fluid consistency when stirred.
5. Stir in the honey, vanilla, and salt into the almond butter mixture.
6. Now add the liquid mixture to your dry mix and combine well.

7. Into the bowl add the chopped apricots.
8. You can add the coconut in at this time if you chose to use it or you could use the coconut to coat the top of the bars.
9. Lay parchment paper down in an 8 × 8 inch baking pan.
10. Pat the mixture into the prepared pan with your fingers, making sure it is packed down well.
11. Place in the refrigerator to harden or freezer for at least 1 hour.
12. Cut into pieces and serve.

DINNERS

Beef

ROAST WITH A RUB

Ingredients:

- 1 teaspoon dried oregano
- 1 tablespoon sea salt
- 1 teaspoon garlic powder
- 1 teaspoon black pepper
- ½ teaspoon onion powder
- ½ teaspoon ground cayenne pepper
- 1 tablespoon paprika
- ½ teaspoon dried thyme
- 2 tablespoons olive or coconut oil
- 3 to 4 pound roast (chuck and sirloin tip work well)

Directions:

1. Preheat your oven to 350°F.
2. Line a baking sheet with aluminum foil or use an oven-safe Dutch oven.
3. Begin by mixing the dry spices in a small bowl: oregano, salt, garlic powder, pepper, onion powder, cayenne, paprika, and thyme.
4. Stir in the olive oil and make sure all the ingredients are blended thoroughly.
5. Place the roast on the prepared baking sheet, and cover on all sides with the spice mixture.

6. Roast 1 hour in the preheated oven, or until the internal temperature of the roast reaches 145°F.
7. Allow the roast to rest for 15 to 20 minutes before slicing.

MEATY MEATLOAF

Ingredients:

- ♦ 2 tablespoons coconut oil
- ♦ 1 onion, diced
- ♦ 4 carrots, thinly sliced
- ♦ Salt and pepper to taste
- ♦ ½–1 teaspoon chili powder
- ♦ 2 bell peppers, chopped
- ♦ 1 tablespoon homemade Worcestershire sauce
- ♦ 1 cup medium to hot salsa
- ♦ 3 pounds ground beef
- ♦ 3 eggs, beaten

Directions:

1. Preheat oven to 350°F.
2. In a medium frying pan, heat the coconut oil over medium heat.
3. Add the onions and carrots.
4. Now add salt, pepper, and chili powder.
5. Cook until onion becomes translucent and carrots start to soften.
6. Gently add the bell pepper and sauté until it starts to soften.
7. Add Worcestershire sauce and salsa and cook for another minute or two.
8. Remove from heat and allow to cool slightly.
9. Place the ground beef into a large bowl and add the vegetable mixture and eggs.
10. Mix thoroughly.

11. Place mixture into an 8 × 8 or 9 × 9 baking dish and form into a loaf.
12. Bake in your oven for 1 hour or until the internal temperature of the loaf reaches 160°F.
13. Remove from the oven and allow the loaf to rest a few minutes before slicing.

Homemade Worcestershire Sauce:

Here is a Paleolithic condiment you can make yourself and keep on hand whenever you find a recipe you want to convert to Paleolithic.

- 1 cup apple cider vinegar
- ¼ cup coconut aminos
- ¼ cup Thai fish sauce (optional, but makes it taste great)
- ¼ cup water
- ¼ teaspoon coarse black pepper
- ½ teaspoon dry mustard
- ½ teaspoon onion powder
- ¼ teaspoon ground cinnamon
- ½ teaspoon ground ginger
- ½ teaspoon garlic powder

Directions:

1. Place all the ingredients into a saucepan on your stove top.
2. Bring to a boil and allow it to simmer for 1 to 2 minutes.
3. Cool and store in a container in your refrigerator.

RIBS IN A CROCK

Ingredients:

- 4 pounds beef ribs
- 2 cups diced tomatoes
- 1 (6-ounce) can tomato paste
- 1 teaspoon onion powder
- 1 tablespoon minced garlic
- 1 teaspoon paprika
- 2 teaspoons sea salt
- 1 teaspoon black pepper
- ½ cup raw honey (optional)
- 2 tablespoons homemade Worcestershire sauce
- 1 tablespoon apple cider vinegar

Directions:

1. Turn slow cooker on low.
2. Place ribs into your slow cooker.
3. In a small bowl, mix the diced tomatoes, tomato paste, onion powder, minced garlic, paprika, salt, pepper, honey, Worcestershire, and apple cider vinegar and stir thoroughly.
4. Pour mixture evenly over ribs.
5. Put lid on slow cooker and cook on low for about 8 hours.
6. Remove and serve.

CRUSTLESS PIZZA

Remember, cheeses are *always* optional with these recipes, but I personally can't imagine a "pizza" without them!

Ingredients:

- 2 pounds ground beef
- 2 eggs
- ¼ cup aged Parmesan cheese (optional)
- 2 teaspoons dried oregano
- ½ teaspoon dried onion powder
- 2 teaspoons sea salt
- 2 garlic cloves, finely chopped
- Finely chopped cooked meat as a topping
- ½ cup of 100% tomato sauce
- 1 tablespoon Italian seasoning
- 1 red onion, thinly sliced
- ½ bell pepper, chopped
- 6 to 8 fresh mushrooms, sliced
- Pitted black olives, sliced
- 8 ounces aged cheddar cheese, shredded (optional)

Directions:

1. Preheat oven to 450°F.
2. Lightly grease a lipped cookie sheet or use foil on a cookie sheet, crimping all the way around to create a lip.
3. In a medium bowl, mix the ground beef with the eggs.

4. Add the Parmesan cheese, spices, and garlic and mix until thoroughly incorporated.
5. Spread the mixture onto the cookie sheet and press into desired pizza shape.
6. Place the cookie sheet into the oven and cook 10 to 12 minutes—until meat is thoroughly cooked.
7. Now place your oven to the broil setting.
8. Take your meat pizza and cover it with the tomato sauce.
9. Sprinkle on the Italian seasoning.
10. Top with your veggies and then sprinkle the cheese on top.
11. Place your pizza back into the oven and cook for an additional 4 to 5 minutes or until the cheese is lightly browned.
12. Remove from the oven and allow to cool slightly.
13. Slice and enjoy.

FLAVORFUL BEEF STEW

Ingredients:

- 4 pounds stew meat
- 1 teaspoon sea salt
- ½ teaspoon black pepper
- 2 teaspoons coriander
- 1 teaspoon cinnamon
- Coconut oil for frying
- 1 onion, sliced
- 3 carrots, sliced
- 3 garlic cloves, chopped
- 1 cup chicken broth
- 2 cups beef stock
- 2 bay leaves

Directions:

1. Preheat oven to 350°F.
2. Season meat with salt, pepper, coriander, and cinnamon.
3. In a large ovenproof pot, heat up enough coconut oil on the stove top to cover the bottom of the pot when melted.
4. Place stew meat in the hot oil and brown all sides of the meat.
5. Remove the meat from the pot and set aside.
6. Add a little more oil to the pot and then cook the onion, carrot, and garlic.
7. After several minutes, add the chicken broth, beef stock, and bay leaves.
8. Bring this mixture to a simmer and add the meat back to the pot.
9. Now, place the lid on the pot and transfer the pot to the oven.
10. Cook for 2 to 2½ hours—until meat is tender.
11. Serve up with your favorite sides.

SLOW COOKER CHILI

Ingredients:

- ◆ 2 pounds ground beef
- ◆ 1 tablespoon coconut oil
- ◆ ½ onion, diced
- ◆ 3 celery stalks, diced
- ◆ 2 cloves garlic, sliced
- ◆ 2 teaspoons ground cumin
- ◆ 2 teaspoons chili powder
- ◆ 2 teaspoons thyme
- ◆ 12-ounce jar salsa
- ◆ 8-ounce can diced tomatoes
- ◆ 7 ounce can mild green chilies
- ◆ 2 teaspoons sea salt

Directions:

1. Begin by turning on your slow cooker (low to medium for 8 hours; high for 4 hours).
2. Heat the coconut oil in a pan on top of the stove and add ground beef.
3. Cook for 7 to 8 minutes, until the ground beef is cooked through.
4. Remove from heat and drain the grease from the beef.
5. Transfer the beef to a slow cooker.
6. Add the onions, celery, and garlic.
7. Next, add cumin, thyme, and chili powder.
8. Pour in the salsa, tomatoes, green chilies, and salt over the beef.
9. Put the cover on your slow cooker and cook until finished.

BEEF AND BROCCOLI

Ingredients:

♦ 2 tablespoons coconut oil

♦ 2 cloves of garlic, minced

♦ 1 pound petite sirloin steak, cut into very thin strips

♦ ¼ teaspoon of sea salt

♦ 2 tablespoons lemon juice

♦ 2 teaspoons freshly grated ginger

♦ 2 teaspoons ground black pepper

♦ ½ teaspoon red pepper flakes

♦ ¼–½ cup chicken broth

♦ 2 cups broccoli florets

♦ 2 cups carrots, thinly sliced

♦ 1 green onion, thinly sliced

Directions:

1. In a large skillet, heat the coconut oil and cook the garlic for 3 to 4 minutes.
2. Add the sliced beef and salt and cook until browned.
3. Remove the beef from the pan and turn off the heat.
4. In a small bowl, mix the lemon juice, ginger, pepper, and red pepper flakes with ¼ cup of chicken broth.
5. Turn the flame on again to medium heat under the pan.
6. Add a little more coconut oil if pan is dry.
7. Place the broccoli florets and carrots in the heated pan.
8. Now pour the liquid ingredients from the small bowl on top and toss to coat the broccoli and carrots.

9. Cook over medium heat until the broccoli is tender.
10. Return the beef to the pan and add the green onions.
11. Add the remaining chicken broth if you wish.
12. Stir the beef in until it is coated with sauce and let simmer for a few minutes until the food is heated through.

Poultry

HOMEMADE BUFFALO CHICKEN

Ingredients:

- 2½–3 pounds chicken wings or drumettes
- ½ cup ghee or butter
- 1 teaspoon sweet paprika
- 1 tablespoon apple cider vinegar
- 2 garlic cloves, finely chopped
- 4 tablespoons hot sauce or more if you desire a spicier sauce

Directions:

1. Preheat oven to 450°F or heat up your grill to medium-high heat.
2. Rinse the chicken pieces and pat dry with a paper towel.
3. Heat the ghee in a small saucepan over low heat on the stove top.
4. Stir in the paprika, vinegar, garlic, and hot sauce and blend.
5. Remove from heat.
6. Pour about a quarter of this sauce into a small bowl and pour the remaining sauce into a large bowl and set aside.
7. If you are cooking in the oven, place the chicken pieces on a rimmed baking sheet lined with foil or try placing the chicken on a wire rack set down on the rimmed baking sheet. (This allows the fat to drip down through the rack and away from the chicken, producing crispier chicken.)
8. Take the sauce in the small bowl and brush it over the chicken.

9. If using your grill, cook the chicken pieces over medium-high heat for 12 to 15 minutes.
10. If using the oven, bake for 30 minutes, turning halfway through.
11. Once the chicken is finished cooking in the oven, turn the oven over to broil and broil the wings on each side until they are crispy and dark in color.
12. Dump the cooked chicken pieces into the large bowl with the remaining sauce and stir to coat.

AMAZING CHICKEN FAJITAS

Ingredients:

♦ 2 pounds chicken breasts

♦ 1 teaspoon cumin

♦ 1 teaspoon chili powder

♦ 1 teaspoon ground pepper

♦ Salt to taste

♦ Coconut oil for frying

♦ 3 bell peppers, sliced into strips (one of each color makes attractive dish)

♦ 1 large sweet onion, sliced into strips

♦ 1 medium jicama, peeled and sliced into strips

♦ 3 mangos, peeled and sliced into chunks

♦ 3 avocados, quartered

♦ 2 heads of large lettuce leaves (butter or Bibb lettuce works well)

♦ 1 bunch fresh cilantro, chopped

Directions:

1. Take each chicken breast piece and pound with a meat tenderizer until an even thickness is reached.
2. Take a small bowl and mix the cumin, chili powder, pepper, and salt together.
3. Heat 1–2 tablespoon of coconut oil in a pan and turn flame up to medium heat.
4. Once the oil is hot, sprinkle half the spices directly into the pan.
5. Place the chicken breasts in the pan on top of the spices.
6. Now sprinkle the rest of the mixed spices on top of the chicken.

7. Sear the first side of the chicken for about 1 minute and then do the same to the other side.
8. When the chicken is cooked through, remove from the pan and transfer to a cutting board to slice into strips.
9. In the same frying pan, add the peppers and onions and cook until tender.
10. Once cooked, turn off the heat.
11. Place lettuce leaves on each plate.
12. Then place the cooked peppers and onions mixture and the jicama, avocado, and mango slices.
13. Finish with the strips of chicken on top.

GRILLED CHICKEN BREASTS WITH GARLIC

Ingredients:

- 3 garlic cloves
- 1 cup olive oil
- Juice from 1 lemon
- 1 cup apple cider vinegar
- 4 chicken breasts

Directions:

1. Crush and mince the garlic cloves.
2. Combine the olive oil, lemon juice, and vinegar together in a gallon-sized Ziploc bag.
3. Put the chicken breasts into the bag and seal.
4. Marinate in the refrigerator for 3 hours.
5. Preheat your grill to medium heat about 15 minutes before time to grill.
6. Gently shake off marinade from the chicken and place onto heated grill.
7. Grill until fully cooked.

CHICKEN CASSEROLE

Ingredients:

- ½ cup ghee or 1 stick of butter
- 1¾ cup coconut milk
- 1 teaspoon garlic powder
- ¾ cup aged Parmesan cheese (optional)
- ½ teaspoon sea salt
- ½ onion, chopped
- 3 large eggs
- 3 chicken breasts, cooked and cubed
- 4 cups cauliflower, steamed and chopped
- ½ teaspoon black pepper
- 2 cups broccoli crowns, chopped

Directions:

1. Preheat oven to 375°F.
2. Heat the ghee in a microwave-safe bowl.
3. Add in the coconut milk, garlic powder, Parmesan cheese, salt, onion, eggs, and pepper.
4. Mix with a fork or whisk until thoroughly blended.
5. Add the cooked, cubed chicken and steamed cauliflower and mix all together.
6. Pour into a greased casserole or cake pan.
7. Lightly sprinkle some additional Parmesan cheese on.
8. Bake for 1 hour.
9. Now turn the oven on to broil.
10. Once heated, place the casserole under the broiler for 7 to 8 minutes.

CROCKPOT CHICKEN IN A DIP

If you are not a cheese eater and don't eat dairy, you will probably want to skip this recipe.

Ingredients:

- 2 pounds of chicken breast
- Garlic powder
- Sea salt
- Coarse black pepper
- 1 package of frozen chopped spinach, defrosted and drained
- 1 (14-ounce) can artichoke hearts
- 8 ounces plain Greek yogurt or kefir
- ½ cup aged Parmesan cheese
- ½ cup aged cheddar cheese

Directions:

1. Cut the chicken breasts into bite-sized pieces.
2. Place the chicken strips into a slow cooker.
3. Sprinkle the chicken with garlic, salt, and pepper to your liking and put the lid on. Put cooker on high and cook for 2 hours OR put on low to cook for 4 hours.
4. Once the chicken is cooked, add the spinach, artichoke hearts, yogurt or kefir, Parmesan cheese, and cheddar cheese.
5. Replace lid onto slow cooker for another hour. This allows the cheeses to melt and coat the chicken.
6. Once melted, turn off slow cooker and serve.

TURKEY MEAT TACOS

Ingredients:

- 2 tablespoons chili powder
- 1½ teaspoons cumin
- 1½ tablespoons paprika
- 1 tablespoon onion powder
- 2 teaspoons garlic powder
- 2 teaspoons oregano
- 1 teaspoon red pepper flakes
- ¼ cup of coconut oil
- 3 pounds ground turkey
- ½ cup water
- Romaine lettuce leaves
- Your favorite salsa
- Avocado slices

Directions:

1. In a small bowl, combine the chili powder, cumin, paprika, onion powder, garlic powder, oregano, and red pepper flakes.
2. In a large skillet, heat the coconut oil.
3. Add the ground turkey and cook until browned.
4. Do not drain liquid!
5. Now shake about ⅓ of the spice mixture into the turkey and stir thoroughly.
6. Repeat the above step two more times until all the spices are incorporated into the turkey.
7. Add ½ cup of water into the turkey and spices.

8. Bring to a boil.
9. Now reduce the heat, and let it cook for about 15 minutes, which will reduce the amount of liquid.
10. Remove from the stove top and allow it to sit for 8 to 10 minutes.
11. While the turkey is resting, line your plate with a lettuce leaf.
12. Now place some of the turkey mixture onto the lettuce leaf, followed by some salsa and avocado slices (if desired).

HUNTER'S CHICKEN

Ingredients:

- 3 tablespoons olive or coconut oil
- 3 pounds chicken
- ½ teaspoon sea salt
- ½ teaspoon coarse black pepper
- 1 medium onion, sliced
- ½ pound sliced mushrooms
- 3 cloves garlic, minced
- 16-ounce can diced tomatoes
- 8-ounce can 100% tomato sauce
- 1 teaspoon dried oregano
- 1 bell pepper cut in large cubes

Directions:

1. In a large skillet, heat coconut oil over medium heat.
2. Season the chicken with salt and pepper.
3. Add the chicken pieces and brown them on all sides.
4. Remove the chicken and drain on paper towels.
5. Add the onions and mushrooms to the hot pan and cook until tender.
6. Now add the garlic, tomatoes, tomato sauce, oregano, and cubed bell pepper.
7. Return the chicken to the frying pan and bring to a boil.
8. Once a boil has been reached, reduce the heat, cover with a lid, and simmer for approximately 30 minutes.
9. Once chicken is done and tender, enjoy!

Pork

MEATY DINNER MUFFINS

Ingredients:

- 14.5-ounce can Italian tomatoes, drained
- 1 onion, peeled
- ½ teaspoon sage
- ½ teaspoon thyme
- ⅛ teaspoon ground nutmeg
- ¼ teaspoon onion powder
- ½ teaspoon ground pepper
- ½ pound ground turkey
- 2 pounds ground beef
- 1 egg
- 1 teaspoon garlic powder
- 1 tablespoon Italian seasonings
- Salt and pepper to taste

Directions:

1. Preheat your oven to 375°F.
2. Lightly grease muffin pans with coconut oil.
3. Place drained tomatoes in a food processor along with the onion.
4. In a small bowl, combine the sage, thyme, nutmeg, onion powder, and pepper together and mix thoroughly.

5. In a large separate bowl, mix this seasoning mix into the ground turkey thoroughly to create "sausage."
6. Now add the beef, egg, garlic, seasonings, salt, and pepper and the tomato/onion puree in with the ground turkey.
7. Take small hunks of meat and form into meatballs that will fit into each muffin tin.
8. Place in the preheated oven for 25 to 30 minutes.
9. Check for doneness.

AROMATIC PORK LOIN

Ingredients:

- 4 large carrots, peeled and sliced
- ½ teaspoon cinnamon
- ¼ teaspoon cloves
- ¼ teaspoon nutmeg
- ¼ teaspoon ground ginger
- ¼ teaspoon black pepper
- 2 garlic cloves
- ½ teaspoon sea salt
- 2 tablespoons olive or coconut oil
- 1½ pound pork loin
- 1½ cups water

Directions:

1. Prepare a slow cooker by placing the sliced carrots in the bottom and turning the heat to high for 3½ hours. (A low setting will require 6 hours of cooking time.)
2. Mix together cinnamon, cloves, nutmeg, ground ginger, black pepper, garlic, and salt.
3. Rub 1 tablespoon of the olive oil all over the pork loin.
4. Now massage the spices over the pork loin.
5. Place a frying pan on a high heat with the remaining olive oil in the bottom.
6. Brown the pork loin on all sides.
7. Remove the pork and place it in the bottom of a slow cooker.
8. Return to the frying pan on the stove and add the water and heat briefly.
9. Now transfer the water from the frying pan to the slow cooker.
10. Put the lid on the slow cooker and cook for the needed amount of time to reach tenderness.

SLOW AND EASY JAMBALAYA

Ingredients:

- ◆ 5 cups chicken stock
- ◆ 4 bell peppers, chopped
- ◆ 1 large onion, chopped
- ◆ 2 garlic cloves, diced
- ◆ 28-ounce can of diced tomatoes—do NOT drain
- ◆ 2 bay leaves
- ◆ ½ pound diced chicken
- ◆ 3 tablespoons Cajun seasoning
- ◆ ¼ cup Frank's Red Hot sauce or hot sauce of your choice
- ◆ 1 pound large shrimp, raw and deveined
- ◆ 1 pound spicy Andouille nitrite/nitrate-free sausage (optional)
- ◆ 1 head of cauliflower
- ◆ 2 cups okra

Directions:

1. Start by putting the chicken stock, bell peppers, onion, garlic, diced tomatoes with juice, bay leaves, chicken, Cajun seasoning, hot sauce, and bay leaves into a slow cooker set on low (6 hour setting).
2. Half an hour before the slow cooker is finished, toss in the sausage.
3. Place the cauliflower into a food processor and pulse until it resembles rice.
4. Add this "rice," raw shrimp, and okra to the slow cooker.
5. Mix ingredients together and continue cooking until shrimp is done and vegetables are tender.

BREAKFAST CASSEROLE FOR DINNER

Ingredients:

- 1 small bunch of dark greens (spinach, Swiss chard, or kale with stems removed)
- 1 teaspoon sage
- 1 teaspoon thyme
- ¼ teaspoon ground nutmeg
- ½ teaspoon onion powder
- 1 teaspoon ground pepper
- 1 pound ground turkey
- Coconut oil or butter for frying
- 10 eggs
- Small bunch of parsley

Directions:

1. Preheat your oven to 375°F.
2. If necessary, wash the greens and then cut into thin strips.
3. In a medium bowl, combine the sage, thyme, nutmeg, onion powder, and pepper and mix thoroughly.
4. Add the ground turkey to the seasonings and mix until combined thoroughly.
5. Place your frying pan over medium heat with coconut oil or butter.
6. Once the oil is hot, place the greens into the pan and sauté for several minutes.
7. Then break up the ground turkey as you add it to the greens.
8. Continue to sauté until the turkey is cooked then remove from heat.
9. In a bowl, whisk the eggs and add the cooked, greens and turkey mixture.

10. Pour everything into a greased 8 × 8 pan and place in preheated oven.
11. Bake for 20 to 25 minutes—until the center is firm when jiggled.
12. Remove the pan from the oven and allow to cool slightly before cutting into squares.

SPICY ITALIAN PORK

Ingredients:

- 1½ tablespoons sea salt
- 1 teaspoon pepper
- ½ teaspoon cumin
- 1 tablespoon garlic powder
- Juice of one lime
- 3–4 pounds pork roast (picnic or butt piece)
- 12 whole cloves
- 1 onion, sliced

Directions:

1. Preheat the oven to 250°F.
2. In a small bowl, mix together the salt, pepper, cumin, and garlic.
3. Mix the juice of the lime with the seasonings.
4. Rub the mixture all over the pork.
5. Now take a sharp knife and slice 6 thin cuts into the pork.
6. Place 2 whole cloves inside each slit.
7. Place the roast into a lightly greased roasting pan with the onion slices on the bottom.
8. Cover with a lid or aluminum foil and roast for approximately 4 hours, or until the middle of the roast reads 160 degrees with a meat thermometer.
9. Let the roast rest for about 20 minutes and then uncover.
10. Use the juice in the bottom of the pan to further moisten the meat if desired.
11. Enjoy!

PORK AND PEPPERS IN A POT

Ingredients:

- 4 large bell peppers
- 1 large onion
- 2 carrots
- 4 cloves of garlic
- ½ head of cauliflower
- 2 pounds ground pork (or a combination of pork and beef)
- 1 (6-ounce) can of tomato paste
- 1 tablespoon dry oregano
- 1 tablespoon dry or fresh tarragon
- Salt and pepper to taste
- ½ cup water

Directions:

1. Start your slow cooker on the low setting.
2. Now cut the tops off the peppers and clean the seeds out.
3. Add the onion, carrots, garlic, and cauliflower into a food processor or finely chop with a knife.
4. In a big bowl, combine the ground pork, shredded vegetables, tomato paste, oregano, tarragon, salt, and pepper to taste.
5. Stuff the peppers with the meat mixture.
6. Arrange the peppers into a slow cooker by having them next to each other so they remain upright.
7. Place any leftover meat down around the peppers.
8. Add the water gently into the bottom of the slow cooker.
9. Cover and cook on low for 8 to 10 hours.

PORK LOAF

Ingredients:

- 1 pound ground pork
- 1 egg, beaten
- 4 tablespoons almond flour
- 1 cup coconut milk
- 1 teaspoon sea salt
- ½ teaspoon black pepper
- 1 tablespoon coconut oil
- 1 onion, finely diced
- 6 whole mushrooms, sliced

Directions:

1. Preheat your oven to 400°F.
2. Mix the ground pork, egg, almond flour, coconut milk, salt, and pepper in a bowl.
3. Place this mixture into the refrigerator for about 15 minutes.
4. Place a frying pan over medium heat with the coconut oil and heat.
5. Once the oil is hot, add the onion and mushrooms and cook until softened.
6. Bring the meat mixture out of the refrigerator and place the cooked onion and mushrooms into the meat mixture.
7. Pour the mixture into an ungreased baking pan and shape it into a loaf shape.
8. Place the pan into the oven and bake for approximately 1 hour. (Make sure the center is cooked through.)
9. Allow to cool for a few minutes and then slice to desired thickness.

SWEET AND SAVORY PORK CHOPS

Ingredients:

- 4 pork chops with the bone in
- Salt and pepper to taste
- 4 tablespoons coconut oil
- 2 large onions, sliced
- 4 apples, cored and sliced

Directions:

1. Season the pork chops on both sides with salt and pepper.
2. Place a large frying pan over medium heat with 2 tablespoons of coconut oil.
3. Place the pork chops into the heated oil and fry for 5 minutes on each side.
4. Once the pork chops are browned, remove them from the pan and set aside.
5. Reduce the heat under the frying pan to medium-low, add the other 2 tablespoons of coconut oil and allow to heat.
6. Now add the onions and apple slices.
7. Cook until the onions have caramelized and the apple slices are soft.
8. Plate the pork chops on plates and top with the apple and onion mixture.

Seafood & Fish

SHRIMP OVER SPAGHETTI

Ingredients

- 1 spaghetti squash
- 4 tablespoons olive oil
- 4 garlic cloves, minced
- 1 pound shrimp
- Dash of sea salt

Directions:

1. Preheat your oven to 375°F.
2. Take a long sharp knife and cut the squash in half lengthwise.
3. Scrape out the seeds.
4. Brush the flesh of the squash with some of the olive oil.
5. Place the squash face down in a baking dish and cook for 40 to 45 minutes.
6. While the squash is cooking, place half of the olive oil into a frying pan.
7. Over medium heat, sauté 2 cloves of minced garlic in the olive oil until lightly golden.
8. Remove the garlic and oil into a small dish and set aside. (This will be used to toss in with the finished squash.)
9. When the spaghetti squash is finished cooking, allow it to cool slightly so you don't get burned when you work with it.
10. While the squash is cooling, place the other 2 tablespoons of olive oil into the frying pan and heat.

11. Place the other 2 cloves of minced garlic and shrimp in the pan and cook until the shrimp is cooked.
12. Turn off the heat under the frying pan when finished.
13. Taking a fork, scrape out the flesh of the squash into a large bowl. (It will resemble spaghetti.)
14. Mix the reserved olive oil and garlic mixture into the spaghetti.
15. Place the "spaghetti" on serving dishes and top with the shrimp.

SALMON WITH A TWIST OF LEMON

Ingredients:

- Juice of one lemon
- 1 teaspoon lemon zest
- 2 tablespoons walnut oil
- 1 teaspoon dried dill
- 2 garlic cloves, minced
- 4 salmon fillets, fresh or thawed
- Sea salt

Directions:

1. Place the lemon juice, lemon zest, walnut oil, dried dill, and garlic cloves in a bowl and mix well.
2. Pour the ingredients into a gallon-sized Ziploc bag.
3. Place the salmon fillets into the Ziploc bag and marinate for 1 hour.
4. Preheat your oven to 450 degrees.
5. Take the salmon fillets out of the bag and place on an ungreased baking sheet with the skin side down.
6. Dust the salmon fillets with salt.
7. Cook the salmon in the middle of the oven for 15 to 20 minutes.
8. Remove from the oven.
9. Remove the skin from the salmon and enjoy.

DOUBLE MEAT GUMBO

Ingredients:

- 2 tablespoons olive oil
- 1 onion, finely chopped
- 8 ounces mushrooms, finely chopped
- 1 pound boneless skinless chicken, cubed
- 4 tablespoons lime juice
- 3 tablespoons lemon juice
- ½ teaspoon basil
- ½ teaspoon oregano
- ½ teaspoon thyme
- 1 tablespoon minced garlic
- 1 (6-ounce) can of tomato paste
- ¼ cup of sun-dried tomatoes
- 1 pound cooked shrimp

Directions:

1. Place a deep frying pan over medium heat and add the olive oil to the pan.
2. Place the chopped onion, mushrooms, and the chicken cubes into the pan and stir.
3. Add the lime and lemon juice, as well as the spices and garlic to the pan.
4. Stir well and then cover with a lid and simmer for approximately 12 to 15 minutes, stirring occasionally.
5. When the onions are soft and the chicken is cooked, add in the tomato paste and dried tomatoes.
6. Continue stirring until a sauce is created.

7. Reduce the heat under the pan, and allow to cook for 10 to 15 minutes, stirring occasionally.
8. Finally, stir in the shrimp and simmer.
9. Once the shrimp is cooked, serve into bowls.

LEMON PEPPER FISH

Ingredients:

- ♦ 2 white fish fillets
- ♦ 1 teaspoon pepper
- ♦ Juice from ½ lemon
- ♦ 8 lemon slices
- ♦ Ghee or butter for seasoning

Directions:

1. This dish is prepared in a steamer, so begin to bring the water in the pot to a boil.
2. Cut two pieces of foil and make each piece big enough that it will totally encase a fish fillet.
3. Place a fish fillet on each piece of foil.
4. Sprinkle the pepper on the fish, pour the lemon juice over each piece, and top each piece of fish with 4 thin lemon slices.
5. Place some thin slices of butter on each fish to your liking.
6. Now wrap up each piece of fish in the foil and seal the ends.
7. Place the foiled pieces of fish into the steamer top and cook for 20 minutes.
8. Carefully unwrapped each fish fillet and enjoy with a side dish of vegetables or salad.

NUTTY FLOUNDER

Ingredients:

- 4 eggs
- 1 cup pecans, ground into a meal using a food processor or blender
- 6 white fish fillets, defrosted
- 1 teaspoon sea salt
- ½ teaspoon pepper
- ¼ teaspoon garlic powder

Directions:

1. Preheat your oven to 400°F.
2. While the oven is preheating, crack the eggs into a bowl suitable for dipping the fillets into and whip.
3. Mix the pecan meal with the salt, pepper, and garlic powder.
4. Pour the pecan mixture onto a large plate.
5. Dip each piece of fish into the egg mixture and then coat each side of the fish with the pecan meal.
6. Carefully place each piece of fish into a large baking dish.
7. After all fish is in dish, put any remaining pecan meal on top of the fish and pat it down.
8. Place the baking dish into the oven and bake for 15 to 20 minutes. Make sure the fish is cooked through and starts to flake.
9. Serve and enjoy.

YUMMY CRAB CAKES

Ingredients:

- 1 pound crabmeat—fresh or canned
- 2 tablespoons diced red onion
- 2 tablespoons homemade Paleolithic mayo
- 1 teaspoon minced garlic
- Salt and pepper to taste
- ⅛ teaspoon of cayenne pepper
- 1 egg
- 2 tablespoons coconut flour
- 3–4 tablespoons coconut oil

Directions:

1. Place the crabmeat into a medium-sized bowl.
2. Add the onion, mayo, garlic, salt, pepper, cayenne pepper, egg, and flour.
3. Mix thoroughly but gently so you do not cause the crabmeat to fall apart.
4. In a large skillet, heat the coconut oil over medium heat.
5. Divide the mixture into 10 equal portions and form into patties.
6. Fry for approximately 2 to 3 minutes on each side and allow the cakes to brown.

COLORFUL SHRIMP SALAD

Ingredients:

- 1 pound shrimp, cooked and peeled
- 3–4 ripe avocados, peeled and chopped into ½-inch chunks
- 3–4 ripe tomatoes, chopped
- 2–3 green onions, finely chopped
- 1 orange bell pepper, chopped
- 1 jalapeno pepper, seeded and finely chopped
- 3–4 garlic cloves, minced
- Juice of 2 limes
- Olive oil
- Fresh cilantro leaves, chopped
- Salt and pepper to taste

Directions:

1. Take a large bowl and mix the shrimp, avocados, tomatoes, onions, bell pepper, jalapeno pepper, and garlic together gently.
2. Squeeze the lime juice and olive oil over the top of the salad.
3. Sprinkle the salad with fresh cilantro and season with salt and pepper to your liking.
4. Mix gently.

NUTTY BAKED SALMON

Ingredients:

- 1 pound salmon fillet with skin on
- ½ cup almond meal
- ½ teaspoon ground coriander
- ½ teaspoon ground cumin
- Juice from 1 lemon
- Salt and pepper to taste
- Coconut oil
- Fresh cilantro (optional)

Directions:

1. Preheat the oven to 350°F.
2. In a small-sized bowl, add the almond meal, coriander, and cumin and mix together.
3. Squeeze the juice from the lemon over the salmon fillets and season with salt and pepper.
4. Coat both sides of each fillet with the almond meal mixture.
5. Place the fillets skin side down on a broiler pan that has been lightly greased with coconut oil.
6. Bake for 12 to 15 minutes, making sure the salmon flakes easily with a fork.
7. Top with freshly chopped cilantro before serving if desired.

APPETIZERS

ROLLED CAKES

Ingredients:

♦ 1 (12-ounce) can of tuna
♦ 1 tablespoon lemon juice
♦ ¼ cup homemade Paleolithic mayonnaise
♦ ½ tablespoon dill weed
♦ Salt and pepper to taste
♦ 2 large cucumbers

Directions:

1. In a small bowl, thoroughly combine the tuna, lemon juice, mayonnaise, dill weed, salt, and pepper.
2. Wash the outside of the cucumbers and towel dry.
3. Using a mandolin slicer, place a cucumber lengthwise and slice.
4. Take a slice of cucumber and place a small amount of tuna mixture onto the end of the cucumber slice and roll like a sushi roll.
5. Continue in this manner until all the tuna mixture is used up.

DELI ROLLUPS

Ingredients:

♦ 1 pound of your favorite cooked meat, sliced

♦ 8 ounces plain Greek yogurt (if you eat dairy)

♦ ½ cup dried unsweetened cranberries

♦ ½ cup pecans or walnuts, chopped

Directions:

1. Take the yogurt and place it in a small mixing bowl.
2. Add the dried cranberries and nuts.
3. Place a piece of meat flat on a plate and spread desired amount of filling at one end of the meat.
4. Roll up like a sushi roll.
5. Slice into bite-sized pieces if desired.

STUFFED BABY BELLAS

Ingredients:

- 16 baby bella mushrooms
- ¼ cup bell pepper, chopped
- 2 garlic cloves, minced
- 1 onion, chopped
- Zest from one lemon
- 10-ounce box frozen spinach, defrosted and drained
- ¼ cup chopped nuts (almonds, pecans, walnuts)
- 1 cup aged shredded cheese (optional)
- Salt and pepper to taste
- ¼ cup olive oil and vinegar dressing
- 2–3 tablespoons olive oil

Directions:

1. Begin by preheating your oven to 375°F.
2. Next, remove the stems from the mushrooms and chop them up.
3. In a large saucepan, heat 1 tablespoon of olive oil over medium heat.
4. Add the bell pepper, garlic, onion, and cook for 5 minutes.
5. Reduce the heat and add the lemon zest, spinach, nuts, ½ cup cheese, salt, pepper, and dressing.
6. Cook until mixture is thoroughly heated.
7. Lightly brush olive oil inside the caps of each mushroom and place them into a lightly greased baking dish with sides.
8. Place a heaping spoonful of filling into each mushroom cap and sprinkle with the remaining cheese.

9. Place the baking dish into your preheated oven for 20 minutes and cook until mushrooms are tender.

FRUIT SALAD WITH CINNAMON

Ingredients:

- ◆ 1 large orange, peeled and diced
- ◆ 1 apple, diced
- ◆ 2 spears fresh pineapple, cubed
- ◆ 6–8 large strawberries, tops removed and sliced
- ◆ ½ cup pecans or walnuts, chopped
- ◆ ½ teaspoon ground cinnamon
- ◆ ½ cup shredded unsweetened coconut (optional)

Directions:

1. Place the cut fruit into a medium bowl.
2. Sprinkle with chopped nuts and cinnamon.

AVOCADO DEVILED EGGS

Ingredients:

- 4 eggs, hard-boiled
- 1 avocado, pitted and cubed
- 2 teaspoons hot sauce
- 1 teaspoon lemon juice
- Salt and pepper to taste

Directions:

1. Peel the hard-boiled eggs and cut in half lengthwise.
2. Spoon out the yolks and place the yolks and avocado cubes into a small bowl.
3. Take a fork and mash the egg yolks and avocado into a paste.
4. Add the hot sauce, lemon juice, salt, and pepper and mix thoroughly.
5. Refill the egg whites with the yolk mixture.

BAKED SWEET POTATO FRIES

Ingredients:

- 3 large sweet potatoes
- ¼ cup olive or coconut oil
- 1 tablespoon sea salt
- 2 teaspoons pumpkin pie spice
- 2 teaspoons Cajun seasoning

Directions:

1. Preheat your oven to 500°F.
2. Peel the sweet potatoes and cut off the ends.
3. Cut the potatoes in half lengthwise and to your desired length to make sticks or slice the potatoes into rounded disks.
4. Place the sweet potatoes into a large bowl and add the oil.
5. Mix well to moisten the potatoes with oil.
6. In a small bowl, combine the salt, pumpkin pie spice, and Cajun seasoning.
7. Mix thoroughly.
8. Sprinkle the spices into the bowl with the potatoes and use your hands to mix well.
9. Place a rack on top of a baking sheet.
10. Spread the sweet potatoes out into a single layer on the rack. This will allow the heat to circulate around the potatoes so turning is not required.
11. Bake for 25 to 30 minutes, until browned.
12. Let the potatoes cool for a few minutes before serving.

EASY SHRIMP KABOBS

Ingredients:

- ¼ cup sesame seed oil
- 2 teaspoons lemon juice
- 1 tablespoon minced garlic
- ¼ teaspoon pepper
- 1 pound shrimp, peeled

Directions:

1. In a medium-sized bowl, add oil, lemon juice, garlic, and pepper.
2. Mix thoroughly.
3. Place the marinade in a large Ziploc bag.
4. Rinse the shrimp and towel dry.
5. Place the shrimp inside the Ziploc bag and place in the refrigerator for at least two hours.
6. Heat up your grill to medium heat.
7. While the grill is heating, place shrimps on individual skewers.
8. Once your grill is hot, place the skewers on the grill.
9. Cook the shrimp for 5 minutes or until the shrimp turns pink. (Do not overcook or the shrimp will become tough.)
10. Serve and enjoy!

GARLIC HUMMUS

Ingredients:

- 2 tablespoons olive oil
- 2 teaspoons ground cumin
- ¼ teaspoon sea salt
- ⅛ teaspoon black pepper
- 1 head cauliflower, cored and cut into 1½ inch florets
- ½ cup guacamole
- 3 cloves garlic, smashed into a paste
- Juice of 1 lemon
- ⅛ teaspoon paprika

Directions:

1. Preheat your oven to 500°F.
2. In a large bowl combine the olive oil, cumin, salt, and pepper.
3. Add the cut cauliflower to the bowl and toss to coat the cauliflower with the spices.
4. Transfer the cauliflower to a baking sheet and spread out evenly.
5. Bake for 25 to 30 minutes, stirring occasionally.
6. While the cauliflower is baking, combine the guacamole, garlic paste, and lemon juice.
7. Place the spices and the cauliflower into a food processor and blend until you achieve a smooth paste consistency. (If the paste is too thick, add more olive oil a little at a time until desired consistency is reached.)
8. Season with salt and sprinkle paprika on top.

BACON-WRAPPED SCALLOPS

If you don't eat bacon, you will want to skip this recipe.

Ingredients:

- ¾ cup pure maple syrup
- ¼ cup coconut aminos
- 1 tablespoon spicy mustard
- 12 slices bacon, cut in half
- 12 large sea scallops, halved
- 24 toothpicks
- 2 tablespoons coconut sugar (optional)

Directions:

1. In a medium-sized bowl, mix the maple syrup, aminos, and mustard.
2. Add the scallops and toss to coat them with the sauce.
3. Cover the bowl with plastic wrap, place in the refrigerator, and allow to marinate for 1 hour.
4. Preheat your oven to 375°F.
5. Line a rectangular baking sheet that has a rim with foil.
6. Arrange your bacon pieces on the baking sheet. Do not allow them to overlap.
7. Place the baking sheet into your preheated oven for 10 minutes.
8. Remove the sheet from the oven and pour off the bacon grease.
9. When the bacon is cool enough for you to handle, wrap a piece of bacon around each scallop and secure with a toothpick.
10. Put the bacon-wrapped scallops onto the baking sheet.
11. Sprinkle with the coconut sugar if desired.
12. Place the baking sheet back into the oven for 15 minutes.
13. When the scallops are opaque and the bacon is crisp, your appetizer is ready to be enjoyed.

EASY HOT WINGS

Ingredients:

♦ 2 tablespoons coconut oil

♦ 10 pounds chicken wings

♦ Sea salt

♦ Chipotle powder or cayenne pepper

Directions:

1. Preheat your oven to 525°F.
2. Line two large baking sheets with foil.
3. Now lightly grease the foil with coconut oil.
4. Arrange the chicken pieces onto the foil, spreading them out so they don't lie on top of each other if possible.
5. Cook for 30 minutes and then rotate the positions of the baking sheets.
6. Bake for an additional 30 minutes, until the chicken pieces are browned and crispy.
7. Sprinkle the cooked wings with chipotle or cayenne pepper as soon as you take them out of the oven.
8. Allow the chicken pieces to rest for several minutes.
9. Serve warm if you like crunchy wings or at room temperature if you like softer, chewier wings.

SWEET POTATO SKINS

If you don't eat dairy, you will probably want to skip this recipe.

Ingredients:

- 4 large sweet potatoes, baked
- 3 tablespoons olive or coconut oil
- 1 tablespoon shredded aged Parmesan cheese (optional)
- ½ teaspoon sea salt
- ¼ teaspoon garlic powder
- ¼ teaspoon paprika
- ⅛ teaspoon pepper
- 1½ cups shredded aged cheddar cheese (if you eat dairy)
- ½ cup sour cream (if you eat dairy)
- 4 green onions, sliced

Directions:

1. Preheat your oven to 475°F.
2. Begin by cutting your baked sweet potatoes in half lengthwise.
3. Scoop out the pulp, making sure you leave a ¼-inch shell. (Be careful not to pierce through the skin.)
4. Place the potato skins on a greased baking sheet.
5. In a separate bowl add the oil, Parmesan cheese, salt, garlic, paprika, and pepper and combine well.
6. Brush this mixture on both sides of the skins.
7. Place the baking sheet into the oven for 7 to 8 minutes.
8. Remove the baking sheet from the oven so you can turn the skins over.
9. Bake for another 7 to 8 minutes, until the skins are crisp.

10. Sprinkle the cheddar cheese inside the skins.
11. Place back into the oven and cook for another 3 to 4 minutes to allow the cheese to melt.
12. Remove from the oven and top with sour cream and green onions.
13. Serve and enjoy.

FRUITY SALSA

Ingredients:

- 1 mango—peeled, seeded, and diced
- 1 avocado—peeled, pitted, and diced
- 4 medium tomatoes, diced
- 1 jalapeño pepper, seeded and minced
- ½ cup chopped fresh cilantro
- 3 cloves garlic, minced
- 1 teaspoon sea salt
- 2 tablespoons lime juice
- ¼ cup chopped onion
- 3 tablespoons olive or coconut oil

Directions:

1. In a medium bowl, combine the mango cubes, avocado, tomato dices, jalapeño, cilantro, and garlic.
2. Once combined, add the salt, lime juice, onion, and oil.
3. After blending together, place into your refrigerator for approximately 30 minutes before serving.

DELICIOUS FRUIT DIP

Ingredients:

- 1 cup coconut milk
- 1 teaspoon pure vanilla extract
- 2 ripe bananas
- 2 teaspoons coconut flour
- 1½ tablespoons unsweetened cacao powder

Directions:

1. Begin by placing the coconut milk, vanilla, bananas, and flour into a food processor or blender and process until smooth.
2. Pour out half the mixture and add the cacao powder to the half still in the blender or processor.
3. Process again until the mixture is well blended.
4. Separating out the two halves now allows you to enjoy a vanilla-flavored version and a chocolate one.
5. Place in the refrigerator for a period of time if you desire the dip to be thicker.

ARTICHOKE DIP

Ingredients:

- 10-ounce box frozen spinach
- 1½ cups artichoke hearts, chopped
- 2 cups water
- ¼ cup homemade Paleolithic mayonnaise
- ½ cup aged shredded cheese (optional)
- 2 tablespoons lemon juice
- ½ teaspoon red pepper flakes
- 1 teaspoon garlic powder
- ¼ teaspoon sea salt
- ¼ teaspoon black pepper
- Dash cayenne pepper

Directions:

1. Begin by placing the spinach and artichokes in a saucepan with 2 cups of water.
2. Boil until tender.
3. Drain the water from the vegetables but keep the vegetables in the saucepan.
4. Over low heat, add the mayonnaise, shredded cheese, lemon juice, pepper flakes, garlic, salt, and pepper.
5. Stir well.
6. Dip may be served warm or refrigerated in an airtight container.

BACON-WRAPPED ASPARAGUS

If you eat bacon, you will really like this appetizer. You can, however, eliminate the bacon and enjoy the asparagus with just the dip.

Ingredients:

- ◆ 30 asparagus stalks, with hard base removed
- ◆ 10 bacon slices
- ◆ ½ cup Paleolithic mayonnaise
- ◆ 7 teaspoons lime juice
- ◆ 5 teaspoons finely chopped cilantro
- ◆ Salt and pepper to taste

Directions:

1. Preheat your oven to 450°F.
2. Take the asparagus and place them in piles of 3.
3. Wrap a slice of bacon around each bundle and secure the bundle with a toothpick.
4. Using a rimmed baking sheet, place the bundles on the sheet.
5. Season to your liking with the salt and pepper.
6. Place the baking sheet into the oven and cook for about 20 minutes.
7. While the bundles are cooking, combine the mayonnaise, lime juice, cilantro, salt, and pepper.
8. Once the bundles are cooked, remove from the oven and serve with the flavored mayonnaise.

PIZZA BITES

Ingredients:

- 2 large sweet potatoes, wide in diameter and peeled
- Salsa
- Aged grated cheese (optional)

Topping Options:

- Black olives, sliced
- Bell peppers, thinly sliced
- Mushrooms, sliced
- Green onions, sliced
- Fresh pineapple, thinly sliced and cut into squares

Directions:

1. Preheat your oven on broil.
2. Using a mandolin, thinly slice the sweet potatoes so the slices are round.
3. Lay the potato slices on a baking sheet.
4. Place under the broiler and cook for approximately 5 minutes.
5. Now flip the slices over.
6. Broil for another 4 to 5 minutes, until the slices are crispy.
7. Once they are crispy, remove them from the oven.
8. Place a spoonful of salsa on each potato slice.
9. Top with your favorite ingredients. (Make sure your toppings are mostly cooked and thinly sliced because they won't be in the oven very long.)
10. Place the baking sheet back into the oven on a lower shelf position and let your toppings get hot and allow any cheese to melt. Watch closely so they don't burn.

CROWD-PLEASING MEATBALLS

Ingredients:

Meatballs

♦ 2 eggs

♦ ¼ cup almond flour

♦ 1 tablespoon adobo sauce

♦ 1 teaspoon dried oregano

♦ 1 teaspoon onion powder

♦ 1 teaspoon garlic powder

♦ Salt to taste

♦ 1 pound ground beef

Sauce

♦ 1 cup chicken broth

♦ 15-ounce can 100% tomato sauce

♦ 1 jalapeño pepper, diced

♦ 2 teaspoons dried oregano

♦ 2 teaspoons onion powder

♦ 1 teaspoons garlic powder

♦ Sea salt, if desired

Directions:

1. Preheat your oven to 400°F.
2. In a large bowl, combine the eggs, almond flour, adobo sauce, oregano, onion powder, garlic powder, and salt.
3. Mix thoroughly.
4. Add the ground beef to the mixture and work the spices all through the beef.
5. Form the beef mixture into balls.
6. Place in a lightly greased baking dish that will hold the number of meatballs you've created.
7. Bake in your preheated oven for approximately 15 minutes, until browned.
8. In a saucepan, add the chicken broth, tomato sauce, pepper, oregano, onion powder, garlic powder, and salt.
9. Stir thoroughly and heat over a low heat.
10. Pour over the meatballs when ready to enjoy.

SCRUMPTIOUS GAZPACHO

Ingredients:

- 4 large tomatoes, diced
- ½ red onion, diced
- 1 cucumber, diced
- 1 bell pepper, diced
- 1 bunch, plus ¼ cup fresh cilantro
- 1 small jalapeno, finely chopped
- 2 garlic cloves, minced
- 2 teaspoons ground cumin
- Salt and pepper to taste
- 2 tablespoons apple cider vinegar
- 2 ripe avocados, pitted, peeled, and diced
- ½ cup canned coconut milk
- Juice from ½ lime

Directions:

1. Using a food processor or blender, add the tomatoes, onion, cucumber, bell pepper, bunch of cilantro, jalapeno, garlic, cumin, salt, pepper, and vinegar.
2. Blend until smooth.
3. Pour into a serving bowl and place into the refrigerator until cold.
4. Using a hand mixer, combine the avocado, remaining cilantro, milk, and lime juice.
5. Beat on high until the mixture is smooth and slightly fluffy.
6. Once gazpacho is chilled, top with a spoonful of cream and enjoy.

DESSERTS

Many of these desserts are made with raw honey, dark chocolate, and some dried fruits. Just like the title says, these are desserts and should only be enjoyed occasionally.

BROWNIES

Ingredients:

- 16 ounce jar creamy roasted almond butter
- 2 eggs
- 1¼ cups raw honey
- 1 tablespoon pure vanilla extract
- ½ cup unsweetened cacao powder
- ½ teaspoon sea salt
- 1 teaspoon baking soda
- 1 cup dark chocolate chips (72% or higher)

Directions:

1. Preheat your oven to 325°F.
2. Start with a large bowl and stir the almond butter until smooth.
3. To the butter, add the eggs, honey, and vanilla and mix well.
4. Now add the cacao powder, salt, and baking soda and blend completely.
5. Gently fold in the chocolate chips.
6. Pour the brownie mixture into a lightly greased 9 × 13 inch baking dish.
7. Bake at 325° for 35 to 40 minutes.
8. Allow to cool before slicing.

CARROT CAKE

Ingredients:

Cake

- 1 cup almond butter
- 4 tablespoons pure vanilla extract
- 6 eggs
- 2 teaspoons fresh orange juice
- 8 tablespoons raw honey
- 4–5 cups shredded carrot
- 3 cups unsweetened raisins
- 6 cups almond flour
- 2 teaspoons nutmeg
- 2 tablespoons cinnamon
- 2 teaspoons salt
- 2 teaspoons baking soda
- 2 teaspoons baking powder

Icing

- 1 cup coconut milk
- ½ cup raw honey
- Dash of sea salt
- 2 tablespoons arrowroot powder
- 2 tablespoons water
- 1¼ cups coconut oil

Directions:

1. Preheat your oven to 325°F.
2. In a large bowl, place the almond butter and vanilla and stir until smooth.
3. Add the eggs and combine completely.
4. Now add the orange juice, honey, carrots, and raisins and blend.
5. In a separate bowl, mix together the flour, nutmeg, cinnamon, salt, soda, and powder.
6. Now gently combine the wet ingredients with the dry ones.
7. Take two 9-inch cake tins and lightly grease with coconut or olive oil.
8. Divide the batter evenly between the two pans.
9. Place into your preheated oven and bake for 45 to 50 minutes. (Insert a toothpick or cake tester into the middle of each cake to make sure no liquid is present—only crumbs.)
10. Allow the cake to cool on a rack for approximately 20 minutes before removing the cakes from the pans.
11. In a medium saucepan, add the coconut milk, honey, and salt and stir over medium heat.
12. After blending, reduce the heat, simmer and stir constantly for 10 minutes.
13. Remove from the heat.
14. In a separate bowl, combine arrowroot powder with the water and stir to make a paste.
15. Now stir the arrowroot paste into the coconut milk mixture and heat over medium heat until the mixture thickens.
16. Remove from the heat and place into a bowl that contains the melted coconut oil.
17. Blend thoroughly.
18. Place mixture into a covered container and place in freezer for 45 minutes.
19. Now remove the container from the freezer and stir. Mixture will be thick.
20. Frost your cake with the coconut icing.
21. Garnish with shredded carrots, coconut flakes, and chopped nuts if desired.

NO-BAKE APPLE CRISP

Ingredients:

- 4 apples, chopped
- ½ cup fresh-squeezed orange juice
- ¾ cup pecan halves
- ¾ cup sliced walnuts
- ¾ cup golden raisins
- 1 teaspoon ground ginger
- 1 teaspoon ground cinnamon
- 1 teaspoon nutmeg

Directions:

1. Place the apples into an 8 × 8 inch baking dish.
2. Drizzle the orange juice over the apples.
3. Toss together until the apples are coasted.
4. In a food processor, combine the pecans, walnuts, raisins, ginger, cinnamon, and nutmeg and pulse until coarsely chopped.
5. Spoon the nut mixture over the apple mixture and serve.

BLACKBERRY COBBLER

Ingredients:

- 1 pint fresh blackberries or defrosted, frozen blackberries
- ¼ cup raw honey
- ½ cup almond flour
- ½ teaspoon arrowroot powder
- ½ teaspoon sea salt
- ½ teaspoon baking soda
- 1 teaspoon baking powder
- 1 teaspoon ground cinnamon
- 1 teaspoon ground nutmeg
- ½ cup almond or coconut milk
- 1 teaspoon pure vanilla extract

Directions:

1. Preheat your oven to 350°F.
2. Lightly grease an 8 × 8 inch baking dish with olive oil or coconut oil
3. Place the blackberries in the baking dish and drizzle with the honey.
4. In a separate bowl, mix the almond flour, arrowroot, salt, baking soda, baking powder, cinnamon, and nutmeg.
5. Add the almond or coconut milk and vanilla to the dry ingredients and mix well.
6. If batter is too dry, gently add more milk until a smooth consistency is obtained.
7. Pour the batter over the blackberries and place in the oven.
8. Back for 25 to 30 minutes.
9. Remove from the oven when the crust is browned.
10. Enjoy!

BANANA CHOCOLATE PIE

Ingredients:

Crust

- 1½ cups almond flour
- 5 large dates, finely chopped
- Large pinch of sea salt
- 3 tablespoons coconut oil

Filling

- 5 small bananas, cut into pieces
- 5 large dates, chopped
- 1 cup coconut milk
- ⅓ cup unsweetened cacao powder
- 1 tablespoon pure vanilla extract
- ½ cup sliced almonds
- 2 ounces dark chocolate, chopped

Directions:

1. Preheat oven to 350°F.
2. Lightly grease a 9-inch pie plate with cooking spray or coconut oil.
3. Place the almond flour, dates, and salt into a food processor.
4. Pulse until the dates and almond flour are well combined.

5. Add the oil and continue processing until the mixture starts to come together like a dough. (If the mixture is too dry, add a few more drops of oil until desired consistency is reached.)
6. Bake the crust for 15 minutes or until the crust is browned.
7. Let it cool completely before adding filling.
8. Start to make the filling by combining the bananas, dates, coconut milk, cacao powder, and vanilla into the food processor.
9. Process the mixture until it has a smooth consistency.
10. Pour the mixture into your cooled pie crust and top with your almonds and chocolate pieces.
11. Cover the top with plastic wrap and place in the freezer for a minimum of 4 hours.
12. About 30 minutes before you want to serve it, take the pie out of the freezer, remove the plastic wrap, and allow it to sit at room temperature until it can be sliced.
13. Serve and enjoy!

CHOCOLATE DONUTS

Ingredients:

- 10 pitted dates
- 2 tablespoons water
- 1 tablespoon pure vanilla extract
- 6 eggs
- ½ cup coconut flour
- ½ teaspoon ground cinnamon
- ¼ teaspoon sea salt
- ¼ teaspoon baking soda
- ⅓ cup unsweetened cacao powder
- ½ cup coconut oil, melted
- Melted dark chocolate (72% or higher)

Directions:

1. Preheat your oven to 350°F.
2. Generously grease a donut pan with coconut oil.
3. Taking a microwave-safe bowl, place the dates and water into the bowl and microwave on high for 30 seconds.
4. Remove from the microwave and mash the dates into a paste.
5. In your food processor bowl, add the date paste, vanilla, and eggs.
6. Process the mixture until it is thoroughly combined.
7. Now add the flour, cinnamon, salt, baking soda, cacao powder, and melted oil to the mixture.
8. Mix and occasionally stop the processor and scrape down the sides and reprocess if necessary so the mixture is a smooth consistency.

9. Pour the mixture into the circles of the pan so they are approximately ⅔ full.
10. Place in your oven and bake for 15 to 20 minutes—until the batter is no longer liquid.
11. Remove from your oven and cool the pan on a cooling rack for 15 minutes.
12. Carefully remove the donuts from the pan and allow to cool completely on the rack.
13. Top with melted chocolate or your favorite topping if desired.

C.C.C. BARS

Ingredients:

Crust

- 12 dried dates, pitted and stems removed
- ½ cup almond butter
- ¼ cup shredded unsweetened coconut
- 2 tablespoons raw honey
- 3 tablespoons unsweetened cacao powder
- 1 teaspoon ground cinnamon
- Pinch of sea salt

Caramel

- 12 dried dates, pitted and soaked in water for an hour
- 6 tablespoons canned coconut milk
- 3 tablespoons water
- 1 teaspoon pure vanilla extract
- Pinch of sea salt

Topping

- 1 cup dark chocolate, melted (72% or higher)
- ¼ cup canned coconut milk
- 2 teaspoons ground coffee
- Coarse salt to sprinkle on top

Directions:

1. Begin by lightly greasing a bread pan with coconut or olive oil.
2. Using a food processor, add all the ingredients for making your crust: dates, almond butter, coconut, honey, cacao powder, cinnamon, and a little salt.
3. Once thoroughly combined, pour the mixture into your bread pan and firmly compress into the bottom of the pan with an even thickness throughout.
4. Proceed with making the caramel.
5. Add the dates to the processor and pulse until the dates have broken down. This takes about 45 seconds.
6. Now add the coconut milk a little at a time while the processor is running.
7. Now add the water in the same way.
8. Add the vanilla and a little salt.
9. Continue processing until the mixture resembles caramel. The entire process should take anywhere from 4 to 5 minutes.
10. Once the desired consistency is reached, pour the caramel over the crust and spread evenly.
11. Now take your melted chocolate and add the coconut milk to it.
12. Process in your microwave for 30 seconds to keep the chocolate pourable.
13. Now add the ground coffee and mix well.
14. Pour the mixture over the caramel and gently spread to achieve an even layer.
15. Sprinkle salt on top of chocolate.
16. Place your bread pan into the freezer to allow the chocolate to harden. This should occur after 15 minutes.
17. Slice and enjoy!

CHOCOLATE COCONUT PUDDING

Ingredients:

- 14 ounce can coconut milk
- 3½ cups almond milk
- 7 tablespoons arrowroot powder
- 9 tablespoons unsweetened dark cacao powder
- ½ cup coconut sugar
- 2 teaspoons pure vanilla extract
- Pinch of sea salt
- Shredded, unsweetened coconut for topping

Directions:

1. In a medium saucepan over medium-high heat, place the coconut milk, almond milk, arrowroot, cacao, and sugar and bring to a boil.
2. Allow the mixture to boil for 2 minutes, stirring constantly. (Mixture should end up being thick.)
3. Stir in the vanilla and salt.
4. Pour into dessert bowls.
5. Garnish with shredded coconut.

LEMON BARS

Ingredients:

Topping

- 6 eggs
- ½ cup raw honey
- Juice from 8 lemons (1 cup)
- ½ cup coconut oil
- Shredded unsweetened coconut for topping

Crust

- 1 cup raw almonds
- 1 cup macadamia nuts
- ¼ cup raw honey
- ½ cup coconut oil, melted
- 2 eggs

Directions:

1. Preheat your oven to 400°F.
2. Using a medium saucepan, stir together the eggs, honey, and lemon juice over medium-high heat.
3. Now add the coconut oil.
4. Continue stirring until the mixture thickens and begins to bubble.
5. Remove from heat.
6. Pour mixture into a bowl and place in your refrigerator to cool.
7. Using a food processor, add the almonds and macadamia nuts.

8. Pulse at intervals until you have the nuts in small chunks. Do not process too much or you will have a flour mixture. You want a coarse, chunky texture.
9. Into a mixing bowl, place the nut mixture, honey, melted oil, and eggs and mix thoroughly.
10. Using coconut oil or olive oil, grease a rectangular pan.
11. Spread the mixture into the pan evenly.
12. Bake for 15 to 20 minutes, until the crust is done.
13. Remove from the oven and cool completely.
14. Once the crust is cooled, take your lemon mixture out of the refrigerator and spread over the crust.
15. If desired, sprinkle shredded coconut over the top and return to the refrigerator.
16. Once thoroughly cooled, slice and eat.
17. Keep refrigerated.

PECAN CARAMEL BARS

Ingredients:

Crust

- 1½ cups pecans
- ¼ cup coconut oil, melted
- 1 tablespoon raw honey
- 1 teaspoon pure vanilla extract
- ¾ cup almond flour
- ½ teaspoon baking soda
- ½ teaspoon baking powder
- Pinch of sea salt
- 1 egg, whisked

Topping

- 14 dates, pitted and soaked in water for an hour
- 6 tablespoons canned coconut milk
- 3 tablespoons water
- 1 teaspoon pure vanilla extract
- Pinch of sea salt

Directions:

1. Preheat your oven to 375°F.
2. In your food processor, add the pecans and blend to obtain a meal/flour consistency.
3. Now add the melted oil, honey, and vanilla.
4. Process until you have a butter consistency.
5. Remove the pecan butter from the processor and place into a large bowl.
6. Now add the almond flour, soda, baking powder, and salt.
7. Mix well.
8. Now finish making the crust by adding your egg and blend completely.
9. Lightly grease a bread loaf pan with coconut oil and evenly spread out the crust ingredients into the pan.
10. Place in your preheated oven and bake for 30 minutes. Make sure the center is completely done.
11. When the crust is done, remove it from the oven and allow to cool completely on a cooling rack.
12. Drain the liquid from the dates and place them into the bowl of your food processor.
13. Process the dates for 45 seconds.
14. Add the coconut milk a tablespoon at a time to the dates while the processor continues to run.
15. Now add the water in the same manner.
16. Finally, add the vanilla and a little salt.
17. Continue to process until the mixture is the consistency of caramel.
18. Pour the caramel into a completely cooled crust and distribute evenly.
19. Top with chopped nuts if desired.
20. Cool for 30 minutes in the refrigerator before cutting to eat.
21. Refrigerate any leftovers.

CHEWY CHOCOLATE CHIP COOKIES

Ingredients:

- ¾ cup almond flour
- ¼ cup flaxseed meal
- ¼ cup coconut flour
- ¼ teaspoon sea salt
- ½ teaspoon baking soda
- 3.5-ounce dark chocolate bar, broken into small chunks
- ¼ cup coconut sugar
- 1 tablespoon pure vanilla extract
- ¼ teaspoon almond extract
- ½ cup coconut oil
- 1 egg
- 2 tablespoons arrowroot powder

Directions:

1. Preheat your oven to 350°F.
2. In a medium mixing bowl, combine and mix the almond flour, flaxseed meal, coconut flour, salt, baking soda and chocolate chunks together.
3. In a separate bowl, use a beater to thoroughly mix the sugar, vanilla, almond extract, oil, and egg.
4. Beat until the sugar dissolves and the batter is not gritty.
5. Now add the wet ingredients into the dry ingredients.
6. Mix thoroughly using your beaters.
7. Line a cookie sheet with parchment paper or lightly grease your cookie sheet with coconut oil.

8. Place the dough onto the cookie sheet in the form and thickness you desire. (However you place them on the cookie sheet is how they will look when they are baked.)
9. Cook for 10 to 12 minutes.
10. Remove from the oven when cooked and allow to cool on a cooling rack.

CHOCOLATE CAKE

Ingredients:

Cake

- ¾ cup coconut flour, sifted
- ¼ cup unsweetened cacao powder
- 1 teaspoon sea salt
- 1 teaspoon baking soda
- 10 eggs
- 1 cup coconut oil
- 1 cup raw honey
- 1 tablespoon pure vanilla extract

Icing

- 3.5-ounce dark chocolate bar
- ½ cup macadamia oil

Directions:

1. Preheat your oven to 325°F.
2. In a small bowl, combine the flour, cacao powder, salt, and baking soda and mix thoroughly.
3. In a separate large bowl, use a hand mixer to combine the eggs, coconut oil, honey, and vanilla.
4. Now gradually add the dry ingredients to the wet ones using the hand mixer.
5. When thoroughly blended, pour even amounts of batter into two greased 9-inch round cake pans.

6. Bake in your preheated oven for 35 to 40 minutes, until a toothpick comes out free of liquid when inserted into the middle of each cake.
7. Remove from the oven and allow to cool for 15 minutes on a cooling rack.
8. Remove the cakes from their pans and allow to completely cool.
9. Using a small saucepan over low heat, melt the dark chocolate and mix in the macadamia oil.
10. Pour chocolate into a small bowl and place it in the freezer for approximately 15 minutes.
11. Remove icing from the freezer and beat with your hand mixer on high until fluffy.
12. When the cakes are cooled completely, ice them to your liking.
13. Top with chopped nuts, coconut, or your favorite topping.

COCONUT BARK

Ingredients:

♦ 2 ounces dark chocolate

♦ 1 cup coconut oil

♦ 1 cup coconut flakes

♦ 1 cup pecans

♦ ¼ teaspoon sea salt

Directions:

1. Using a double boiler, place broken pieces of dark chocolate in the top pot.
2. Melt the chocolate.
3. Now stir in the coconut oil until it melts.
4. Add the coconut flakes and pecans into the chocolate.
5. Remove from heat.
6. Line an 8 × 8 pan with parchment paper or grease lightly with coconut oil.
7. Pour the batter into the pan and spread evenly.
8. Sprinkle the salt on top if desired.
9. Place the pan into the freezer for approximately 15 minutes. This will allow the mixture to become solid.
10. Now cut into squares.
11. Enjoy.
12. Store any leftover bark in the freezer.

APPLE CINNAMON CAKE

Ingredients:

- 2 cups almond flour
- ½ teaspoon sea salt
- ½ teaspoon baking soda
- ¼ cup arrowroot powder
- 1 teaspoon cinnamon
- ¼ cup coconut oil, melted
- ½ cup raw honey
- 1 egg
- 1 apple, peeled and diced
- 1 tablespoon pure vanilla extract
- ⅛ teaspoon nutmeg

Directions:

1. Preheat oven to 350°F.
2. In a medium bowl, combine the almond flour, salt, baking soda, arrowroot powder, and cinnamon and mix thoroughly.
3. In a separate bowl, combine the coconut oil, honey, and egg and mix.
4. Mix the dry ingredients into the wet ones gently.
5. Add the diced apple pieces and stir gently to mix in with the batter.
6. Pour the batter into a lightly greased bread loaf pan, or you can use lightly greased muffin tins.
7. Evenly distribute the batter and place in your preheated oven.
8. If making cupcakes/muffins, bake for approximately 15 minutes.
9. If making a loaf, bake for approximately 30 minutes.

10. When fully cooked, remove from the oven and allow to cool on a cooling rack.
11. Enjoy!

CHOCOLATE RASPBERRY TORTE

Ingredients:

- ½ cup raspberries
- 7 large eggs, cold
- 14 ounces dark chocolate
- 14 tablespoons butter
- ¼ cup coconut flour
- 1 teaspoon pure vanilla extract

Directions:

1. Preheat your oven to 325°F.
2. Take your 8-inch spring-form pan and find a baking dish big enough to place the spring-form pan down inside it. Make sure the baking dish has sides high enough to hold water halfway up the sides of the springform pan.
3. Line the bottom of your springform pan with foil and allow the foil to come up the outside of the pan so it is above the water line. This will keep water from seeping into your torte.
4. Lightly grease the inside of your pan with butter.
5. Place the raspberries into a blender or food processor and puree until smooth.
6. Using a mixer, beat the eggs until frothy and doubled in size. (This will take about 6 to 7 minutes.)
7. Place the chocolate and butter into a microwave-safe bowl.
8. At 30-second intervals, melt the chocolate and butter until smooth.
9. Add the coconut flour, vanilla, and half the raspberries to the melted chocolate and stir.
10. Mix in half the frothy eggs into the chocolate mixture.

11. Once combined, add the remaining eggs, stirring until completely blended.
12. Spoon the batter into the springform pan.
13. Now place the pan into your rectangular baking dish.
14. Fill the baking dish with water until the springform pan is covered with water halfway up the sides.
15. Carefully place the dish/springform pan combo into your preheated oven.
16. Bake for 20 to 25 minutes or until the internal temperature of the torte reaches 140 degrees.
17. Turn off the heat to the oven.
18. Allow the torte to stay in the oven for another hour.
19. Remove from the oven and allow to cool completely.
20. Now, remove the sides of the springform pan and invert the torte onto a plate.
21. Remove the foil.
22. Using another plate, invert the torte so it is right-side up.
23. Drizzle the remaining raspberry puree over the torte.

ABOUT THE AUTHOR

Amelia Simons is a food enthusiast, wife, and mother of five. Frustrated with traditional dieting advice, she stumbled upon the Paleolithic lifestyle of eating and has never looked back. Without bothering to count calories or stress about endless hours of exercise, eating the Paleolithic way enabled Amelia and her husband to effortlessly drop pounds and lower their cholesterol.

Amelia now enjoys sharing the Paleolithic philosophy with friends and readers and finding new ways to turn favorite recipes into healthy alternatives.

ADDITIONAL RESOURCES

Be sure to check out my other resources:

Gluten-Free Slow Cooker: Easy Recipes for a Gluten-Free Diet

Paleolithic Slow Cooker Soups and Stews: Healthy Family Gluten-Free Recipes

Paleolithic Slow Cooker: Simple and Healthy Gluten-Free Recipes

Going Paleolithic: A Quick Start Guide for a Gluten-Free Diet

4 Weeks of Fabulous Paleolithic Breakfasts

4 Weeks of Fabulous Paleolithic Lunches

4 Weeks of Fabulous Paleolithic Dinners

4 MORE Weeks of Fabulous Paleolithic Breakfasts

METRIC AND IMPERIAL CONVERSIONS
(These conversions are rounded for convenience)

Ingredient	Cups/Tablespoons/ Teaspoons	Ounces	Grams/Milliliters
Butter	1 cup=16 tablespoons= 2 sticks	8 ounces	230 grams
Cream cheese	1 tablespoon	0.5 ounce	14.5 grams
Cheese, shredded	1 cup	4 ounces	110 grams
Cornstarch	1 tablespoon	0.3 ounce	8 grams
Flour, all-purpose	1 cup/1 tablespoon	4.5 ounces/0.3 ounce	125 grams/8 grams
Flour, whole wheat	1 cup	4 ounces	120 grams
Fruit, dried	1 cup	4 ounces	120 grams
Fruits or veggies, chopped	1 cup	5 to 7 ounces	145 to 200 grams
Fruits or veggies, puréed	1 cup	8.5 ounces	245 grams
Honey, maple syrup, or corn syrup	1 tablespoon	.75 ounce	20 grams
Liquids: cream, milk, water, or juice	1 cup	8 fluid ounces	240 milliliters
Oats	1 cup	5.5 ounces	150 grams
Salt	1 teaspoon	0.2 ounces	6 grams
Spices: cinnamon, cloves, ginger, or nutmeg (ground)	1 teaspoon	0.2 ounce	5 milliliters
Sugar, brown, firmly packed	1 cup	7 ounces	200 grams
Sugar, white	1 cup/1 tablespoon	7 ounces/0.5 ounce	200 grams/12.5 grams
Vanilla extract	1 teaspoon	0.2 ounce	4 grams

OVEN TEMPERATURES

Fahrenheit	Celcius	Gas Mark
225°	110°	¼
250°	120°	½
275°	140°	1
300°	150°	2
325°	160°	3
350°	180°	4
375°	190°	5
400°	200°	6
425°	220°	7
450°	230°	8

ALSO AVAILABLE

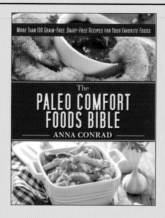

The Paleo Comfort Foods Bible

More Than 100 Grain-Free, Dairy-Free Recipes for Your Favorite Foods

by Anna Conrad

If you think the increasingly popular caveman diet is good for your health but a bit depressing for your taste buds, this is the book that will change your perspective on the paleo diet forever. Now you can enjoy all your favorite comfort foods without sacrificing the terrific health benefits of a grain-free, dairy-free diet.

When chef and caterer Anna Conrad was asked to provide paleo recipes for a fitness group's twenty-eight-day paleo challenge, she was a little skeptical. Could an athlete—or even an average person—really maintain a balanced body without any grains or dairy? Before agreeing to the job, she decided to follow the diet for two weeks to see how she felt. In that short amount of time, she lost eight pounds without feeling hungry or deprived, and her blood pressure, heart rate, and cholesterol all stayed within healthy limits. She gladly provided the recipes and now offers a paleo menu as a regular part of her catering business. In this book, she offers delicious comfort food recipes, including:

- Chicken pot pie
- Creamed spinach
- Meatloaf
- Rueben sandwich
- Shrimp bisque
- Spaghetti carbonara
- And more!

$17.95 Hardcover • ISBN 978-1-62873-620-5

ALSO AVAILABLE

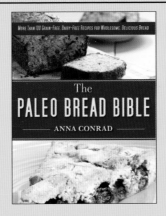

The Paleo Bread Bible

More Than 100 Grain-Free, Dairy-Free Recipes for Wholesome, Delicious Bread

by Anna Conrad

When chef and caterer Anna Conrad was asked to provide paleo recipes for a fitness group's twenty-eight-day paleo challenge, she was a little skeptical. Could an athlete— or even an average person—really maintain a balanced body without any grains or dairy? Before agreeing to the job, she decided to follow the diet for two weeks to see how she felt. In that short amount of time, she lost eight pounds without feeling hungry or deprived, and her blood pressure, heart rate, and cholesterol all stayed within healthy limits. She gladly provided the recipes and now offers a paleo menu as a regular part of her catering business.

But what about bread? How can you make bread without grains? In this book, Conrad teaches how to make wholesome and satisfying breads with almond flour, coconut flour, and a host of other delicious, nongrain flours. Recipes include:

- Almond sandwich bread

- Coconut sandwich bread

- Rosemary and olive oil bread

- Sweet potato rosemary focaccia

- Savory bacon and scallion muffins

- Molasses brown bread

- And many more!

$17.95 Hardcover • ISBN 978-1-62873-619-9

ALSO AVAILABLE

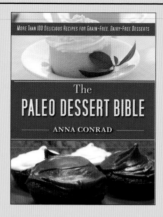

The Paleo Dessert Bible

More Than 100 Delicious Recipes for Grain-Free, Dairy-Free Desserts

by Anna Conrad

By now we all know that the paleo diet yields amazing results for weight loss and overall well-being. But even the most health-conscious among us want to treat ourselves once in a while to something sweet and indulgent. What if we could indulge without cheating on the diet? In this book, readers will find more than one hundred recipes for amazing desserts that will leave you feeling satisfied, energized, and healthy.

When chef and caterer Anna Conrad was asked to provide paleo recipes for a fitness group's twenty-eight-day paleo challenge, she was a little skeptical. Could an athlete—or even an average person—really maintain a balanced body without any grains or dairy? Before agreeing to the job, she decided to follow the diet for two weeks to see how she felt. In that short amount of time, she lost eight pounds without feeling hungry or deprived, and her blood pressure, heart rate, and cholesterol all stayed within healthy limits. She gladly provided the recipes and now offers a paleo menu as a regular part of her catering business. In this book, she offers delicious dessert recipes, including:

- Almond butter cookies
- Bread pudding
- Chewy chocolate cookies
- Chocolate fudge cake
- Lemon squares
- Pecan bars
- And more!

$17.95 Hardcover • ISBN 978-1-62873-621-2

ALSO AVAILABLE

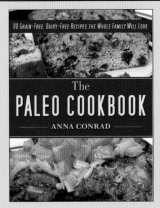

The Paleo Cookbook

90 Grain-Free, Dairy-Free Recipes the Whole Family Will Love

by Anna Conrad

When chef and caterer Anna Conrad was asked to provide paleo recipes for a fitness group's twenty-eight-day paleo challenge, she was a little skeptical. Could an athlete—or even an average person—really maintain a balanced body without any grains or dairy? Before agreeing to the job, she decided to follow the diet for two weeks to see how she felt. In that short amount of time, she lost eight pounds without feeling hungry or deprived, and her blood pressure, heart rate, and cholesterol all stayed within healthy limits. She gladly provided the recipes and now offers a paleo menu as a regular part of her catering business.

In this book, Conrad explains the basics of the paleo diet and then provides ninety delicious recipes for every meal of the day, plus some snacks and desserts. She also includes the menu for her twenty-eight-day paleo challenge for those just starting the paleo lifestyle. Recipes include:

- Pumpkin spice muffins
- Basil pesto stir-fry
- Garlic lime chicken
- Pork tenderloin with apples and onions
- Bison chili
- Baked fish with asparagus and roasted beets
- Stuffed portobellos
- Blueberry citrus pound cake
- And many more!

$17.95 Hardcover • ISBN 978-1-62636-394-6

ALSO AVAILABLE

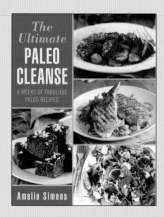

The Ultimate Paleo Cleanse

4 Weeks of Fabulous Paleo Recipes

by Amelia Simons

The first step to becoming healthier can often be the hardest to take. *The Ultimate Paleo Cleanse* helps ease this transition by providing a fantastic starting point with a detailed menu covering breakfast, lunch, and dinner ideas over a four-week period. There's no better way to begin your road to success than with these simple, flavorful meals.

Within *The Ultimate Paleo Cleanse*, readers will find a wide range of recipes covering every meal from breakfast to lunch and dinner, including scrumptious grain-free, gluten-free appetizers and desserts. Some of the delicious choices you'll find in this collection are:

- Delicious quiche cups

- Hearty sautéed peach salad

- Grilled chicken breasts with garlic

- Garlic hummus

- Chocolate coconut pudding

- And many different muffin, bread, and pancake recipes!

Also included in this cookbook is an overview of the paleo lifestyle that will give you a quick, easy-to-follow guide of the recommended foods and the ones to avoid. Improving your health has never been easier!

$17.95 Hardcover • ISBN 978-1-62914-552-5